# SHELTER for the SPIRIT

## CREATE YOUR OWN HAVEN IN A HECTIC WORLD

### Victoria Moran

HarperPerennial

*A Division of HarperCollinsPublishers*

*To my family and my extended family*

Copyright acknowledgments appear on page 222.

A hardcover edition of this book was published in 1997 by HarperCollins Publishers.

HarperCollins books may be purchased for educational, business, or sales promotional use. For information, please e-mail the Special Markets Department at SPsales@harpercollins.com.

First HarperPerennial edition published 1998.

*Designed by Joseph Rutt*

---

The Library of Congress has catalogued the hardcover edition as follows:

Moran, Victoria, 1950–
    Shelter for the spirit : how to make your home a haven in a hectic world / Victoria Moran. — 1st ed.
            p.     cm.
    Includes bibliographical references and index.
    ISBN 0-06-017415-3
    1. Spiritual life. 2. Home—Religious aspects. 3. Home—psychological aspects. I. Title.
HQ734.M824  1997
640—dc20                                                                96-32532

---

ISBN 0-06-092922-7 (pbk.)

16  ❖/RRD  30  29  28  27  26  25

# Contents

# Acknowledgments

Just as many people have put life into my home, many have put something of themselves into this book. They include my agent, Patti Breitman, who did far more than any agent is expected to, because she is also my friend; my most literate editor, Peternelle van Arsdale; her assistant, Kristen Auclair; and everyone at HarperCollins who had a hand in this project.

I wish to thank Dana Guthrie for her excellent research and editorial assistance; Pete Shifflett for his tireless help with computer complexities, and Stan Rosenfeld and Michael Manard for their computer expertise as well; Kevin Kelly for initial editing; Guru Parwaz Khalsa for a wealth of input for the "Cooking" chapter and much inspiration besides; the staff of the UMKC Writers' Hotline; and the reference librarians at the Kansas City, Missouri, Public Library, who answered every question I came up with and never told me to stop bothering them.

Appreciation goes to Reverend Pat Williamson, Lois Hamon, Patricia Grantham, and all members of our class at Unity on the Plaza for their belief in this project and their support; John R. van Keppel of the Mid-America Dharma Group for his insights on meditation; Ken and Evelyn Leong of Maharishi Vedic University, Overland Park, Kansas; and Christopher Clark, M.D., Candace and Rogers Badgett, and the entire staff of the Raj Perfect Health Center, Fairfield, Iowa, for their wisdom on both meditation and Ayurvedic cooking techniques; the New Road Map Foundation for their helpful pamphlet *All Consuming Passion*; Shannon Bailey for her knowledge of *feng shui*; Frankie Grady for her hints on filing and organization; Suzanne Hatlestad, Loring Leifer, Marli Murphy, Suzanne Tague, and Ann Wylie for literary guidance; and authors Dan Millman, LouAnn Stahl, Reverend Robert Ellsworth, Ph.D., and Reverend Janet Ellsworth, who took time from writing their own books to offer advice for mine.

Thanks to the people who helped with the appendixes, including Sherry Payne, Siobhan DeFeo, and Kati O'Riordan Coulter, who provided me with facts and feelings about home birth; Patrick Farenga of Holt Associates/*Growing Without Schooling*, Helen Hegener of *Home Education* magazine, and Orese Fahey for their insights on homeschooling, as well as Malcolm and Nancy Plent of Unschoolers Network for their informative booklet *Famous Home Schoolers*; home business mentor Barbara Brabec, and Barbara Cunningham, business specialist with the University of Missouri Extension, for information on home business; and home health executive Linda Baker and her husband, consultant Charles Baker, as well as Diane Jones of Hospice Association of America, and Jane Lesher, R.N., M.S.N., C.R.N.H., of Heart of America Family Services for their help on the appendix dealing with hospice.

And for assorted information, inspiration, and invaluable assistance in enabling me to write this book, I wish to thank Linda Adler, Vernita Allen, Val Anderson, Reverend Vern Barnet, D.Min., Adrienne Calvert, Bob Calvert, Warren Carter, Ph.D., Loretta Cohn, Kim Crenshaw, Cate Cummings and Cor van Heuman, Joe Eker, James Filberth, D.C., Marcia Fisher, Cynthia Fitting, Necia Gamby, Susan Gibbs, Evelyn Gorten, Nancy Harmon, Esther and Dan Hughes, Kellee Kadillac-Hinkle, Roseanne Penner Kaufman, Bibi and Zadi Khalsa, Jagat Guru Khalsa, Dawn Kimble, Reverend Max

Lafser, Gladys Lawler, Crystal Leaman, Ashley Lynn, Anne-Sophia Marshall, Helene Martin, Robert McWilliams, Reverend Chris Michaels, Rita Moran, Robert Morris, Reverend David Nelson, D.Min., Jan and Bill Pierce, Sonnet Pierce, Carmen Quinton, Rebecca Pryor, Toni and John Rader, Jamie Rich, Diann Roche, Mary and Terry Rouse, Rita Rousseau, Dolores Sehorn, Carol Shifflett, Jolie Simons, Stan Slaughter, Julie Stuffelbeam, Greg Tamblyn, Juanell Teague, Susan Timmerman, Reverend Duke Tufty, Richard Vandever, Jacque White, Carol Wiesner, and Rabbi Michael Zedek.

And thank you, Rachael, for all your ideas and suggestions, as well as putting up for so long with a demanding sibling named "the book," and showing me how special a home can be.

# Foreword

We live in a time when the ordinary life is more elusive than the extraordinary. Some days I'm overcome by feelings of nostalgia for the days when people seemed deeply and satisfyingly engaged in their ordinary activities. Today we seem hungry for new information, extraordinary salaries, and celebrity of every description. Even the average person tries to share, if only partially, in the excitement of these wonders. Something in the human imagination clearly enjoys the thrill of the extraordinary, but something else deep in the soul is profoundly pleased and calmed with everyday, humdrum, unremarkable days and situations.

Often it appears to me that many of our problems stem from overlooking the importance of family, children, the land, the neighborhood, and home. As we seek out exotic teachers, books, and programs of personal growth, we are looking for meaning in all the wrong places. As we focus ambitiously on individual progress and enlightenment, our souls may begin to feel starved, and by then we're convinced we need therapy or pills to deal with the resulting depression and other symptoms. The real problem may well be a simple lack of nourishment for the soul, which feeds best on things that nurture the heart and keep ordinary life vibrant.

This prescription is especially suited to feelings of insecurity that come along in almost every person's life. Given the temper of the times, we may think our disturbing sensations of insecurity may go away if only we understood them and then changed our personalities in appropriate ways. But insecurity may call for a more tangible response. What is it that makes us feel secure? Parents, friends, a familiar place, good work, and a real home go a long way toward establishing a secure life. Whatever can help us feel "at home" while on the job, traveling, or in the house can also offer a reassuring sense of being grounded and centered.

It's common knowledge that a house is not always a home and that a home is not always a house. We have to become adept at the heartfelt tasks of making a home—the art of designing, furnishing, maintaining, and living in a house. It may seem too simple to suggest that deep and debilitating anxiety can be cured by making a home, and some might think it unnecessary to teach someone how to live in a house. But in modern times humane living has entered the province of therapeutics, and the simple necessities are generally obscured by our focus on the sophisticated technologies that complicate our work and play.

I welcome this gracefully written book, full of wisdom and sensitivity to the "deep home" that can cure a troubled soul or make an ordinary life enchanted. It's helpful to listen to someone who has thought long and creatively on the everyday task of making the house a home and who can see the importance to the soul in the careful placing of objects and in centered cleaning and fixing. Ordinary chores satisfy primary longings, and in our time we need to be reminded of their importance.

Wired to the media, we may feel pulled out of our homes and

onto the anxious staging of world history, but peace and humanity begin in a home that shelters the heart, the soul, and the spirit; where work and play enjoy a scope and proportion measured by a human scale. Our humanity is not abstract; it is made concrete by the emotional tone of our homes and the human scale of our living.

Shopping, cleaning, and ordinary housework may often feel like drudgery, but they also give pleasure—a sign that they have a place of real significance in the life of the soul. Make our homes with heart and imagination, and a human culture will follow. But neglect the home, giving everything to wandering and adventuring, and the soul will complain in emotional and physical disturbances.

Early in my life I studied the demanding rules of logic and the often incomprehensible abstractions of philosophy. Now I take my pleasure and find traces of meaning in my family and my home— and in reading fine books such as this one that in graceful language show us the way home.

*Thomas Moore*

# Introduction

Human beings need a place to foster an inner life. *Shelter for the Spirit* is about creating such a place from a house or apartment that used to be only a Tudor or a brownstone. It is about reclaiming home as the primary center for our spirituality, our resourcefulness, and the majority of the best moments of our lives. It is a guide to discovering sacred space in the midst of the ordinary, and to realizing that the ordinary has been extraordinary all along.

Home is so fundamental we tend to overlook the degree to which it affects our work, our well-being, and our overall effectiveness. As Margaret Visser writes, "The extent to which we take everyday objects for granted is the precise extent to which they govern and inform our lives." When we are able to consciously experience and appreciate life at home and make changes there to enhance it when we can, we reap the benefits both when we're home and when we're not. Cleaning out a closet, eating in a little more often, snatching a few minutes alone in the morning to sit with our private plans and thoughts and feelings—such small but specific actions increase the beauty, satisfaction, and peace of mind we experience.

If you're like me, you feel more in control of your life when your house is in order. You probably feel happier when objects of sentimental or aesthetic appeal populate your environment. When you have a place where friends easily congregate, you feel supported. When you know that there is some square footage in the universe set aside for you to be comfortable, creative, and leave a legacy with your name on it, you feel secure.

I've learned what it takes for me to be happy at home from the places I've lived—the London bed-sitter I rented at eighteen; modern complex apartments with balconies and trash compactors; and fine houses in their dotage with old wood and lead glass and gas lines behind the ceiling fixtures. I've learned by being home a lot, as a homeschooling mother and a writer working at home, as well as by traveling for long stretches and needing to bring a sense of home along on the journeys. I've also learned by observing the homes of others.

As a child, I did a lot of visiting. There were the suburban ranches of my mother's half dozen siblings, the cool stone and mahogany bungalows of my elderly nanny's seemingly ancient friends, and the tiny tenement flats where I accompanied my father, a doctor, on house calls. The patients who lived there didn't have the money for a hospital stay, but some of them avoided hospitals on principle. "Those are just places to die," I remember hearing from a tiny old woman who had once met Charles Lindbergh and could name the books of the Bible in order. "If the Lord wants to take me, He can come and get me right here where I live."

Unconsciously I began to read those houses and apartments as a palmist would read the lines on a hand. Each dwelling revealed the character of its inhabitants well beyond their financial status or their taste in furniture. Each one had a personality. Sometimes the simplest were the best: They tended to have the most dogs and the most cookies.

Since then, I've learned that anyone claiming four walls and a roof can create a physical environment that is spiritually sustaining. I've visited Tibetan refugee camps in Nepal and India, where every home, however meager, has an elaborate altar. In that culture, home is sacred. The altar is the focal point of the household, and each one I visited had that peaceful yet purposeful feeling we think of as reserved for cathedrals—or at least good libraries.

I resonate to this kind of atmosphere in other people's houses and aim to create it in my own. It isn't difficult, and it doesn't require artistic talent or design training. It can be as easy as bringing in people and plants, ideas and attitudes, books and music that you love. Their essence permeates the rooms, even after the guests have said good-bye or the book is back on the shelf. Making a home that provides this kind of nourishment began for me with understanding that home is of immense significance to our inner lives. The simple act of caring for our dwelling places and those who live there is, when we do it with our full attention, a spiritual practice on par with any religious discipline.

It may indeed be spiritual practice customized for our era, because in this turn-of-the-millennium time, the need to connect our spirituality with our homes is particularly apparent. Perhaps because baby boomers have experienced the transiency of everything else—sex is not what it was in the seventies, money is not what it was in the eighties—we're looking to eternity. We crave something solid, something safe, something to keep. And we want to go home. We want to mark formal occasions there and celebrate holidays there. We want rituals and a place that is our own to observe them. Surveys attest that both men and women now view activities traditionally associated with the homemaker role with increased respect, and we regard the hours spent at home on personal pursuits as "crucial time."

Many of us have been working more than we'd like, running more than we'd planned, and doing more than we ever thought would be expected of us. We too often feel detached from the things we love most: our homes, our families, our solitary time. We instinctively know we need a deeper bond with home and hearth, but we have forgotten how to achieve and sustain that connection. Attempting it can seem overwhelming. It's easier to focus on something else or be somewhere else.

So with the little vacation time we have each year, we might go to Disney World or Las Vegas or the Galápagos Islands, but once we've been there a while, there is only one place that seems appealing: home. When we get back, we expect to discover what English author Robert Southey did when he wrote, "Home—There is a magic in that little word. It is a mystic circle that surrounds comforts and virtues never known beyond its hallowed limits." He saw these special qualities almost two hundred years ago, before the Industrial Revolution caused us as a society to leave home daily in record numbers. Today we crave that "mystic circle" more than ever. We leave home as mere babies to go to preschool, or pre-preschool. We go out to work. We go out to eat. We go to the gym to exercise because we went out to eat. We travel to get away, but we've already been away. More and more of us want to come home, and we want to find more than a collection of possessions when we get there.

It isn't enough to have a place that keeps us warm and shows our friends that we have taste or can afford a decorator—or look as if we do. We want a home where we can relax, create, be with those we love the most, and be alone with ourselves. We want a place where we can process the events of life as a whole, a place where we feel valued, useful, and protected.

So we turn the key in the lock, open the door, and . . . the dog has made so much confetti out of Kleenex that the bedroom floor resembles Times Square on New Year's morning . . . the bathtub faucet is leaking again, and the plumber who fixed it six weeks ago says the warranty was only good for thirty days . . . fresh vegetables age in the crisper, but there's a meeting tonight, and one of the kids has soccer practice. Dinner will come from the microwave or Taco Bell. The "mystic circle" looks more like a double knot.

*Shelter for the Spirit* is an instruction manual for untying that knot. Every home can be a haven—if not always a heaven. Homes are spiritual entities. They do more than simply house us. Collectively, they define what our neighborhoods and communities look like. Their care or lack of care creates areas of beauty or decay. The people who are nurtured—or not nurtured—within them go out to contribute to the world or detract from it.

Although this book venerates home, it does not suggest a fortress mentality of stone walls and moats or even one of those doormats that says, "GO AWAY." Home may be our center and at times our retreat, but we are part of a greater family. Moreover, the comfort we derive from a spiritually rich environment actually deepens the reserves of generosity we have to draw from for friends, strangers, and favored causes. The more fulfilled we feel, the more likely we are to have the energy to give to others.

While things at home may not be perfect, they're familiar, and—leaks and all—this can be the place where giving to yourself and those you love has at least a shot at being top priority. In this place, you show the world your tastes and interests and values, and into this place you're free to invite only those parts of the world you choose to have here. Here you can chart the course of your life, discern the needs of your soul, and provide for them more often than not.

In *Care of the Soul*, Thomas Moore writes, "The soul prospers in an environment that is concrete, particular, and vernacular. It feeds on the details of life, on its variety, its quirks, and its idiosyncrasies." You honor your home when you relish these particulars and allow them to support your growth. The building you live in is inanimate in one sense, but every atom within it is pulsating with life. It has its own story in which you and the people you live with are characters, just as the structure is a silent character in your biography. You provide the opportunity for life to continue in this place. It in turn gives you a place to cultivate your soul—and do the laundry.

# I
# A Loving Foundation

$A$ house can reveal the extent of your assets, but a home reveals the expanse of your heart. Surely some dwellings are grander than others and some neighborhoods more desirable, but a home is judged by different standards than a house is. A house or apartment gets points for being spacious and well groomed, a home for being relaxed and well loved.

Under ideal circumstances, everybody would have a home like this. We would all realize that as unique representations of life itself, we have no choice but to express this identity in creative work, exuberant play, satisfying relationships, and inviting homes. But because most of us are not convinced that we are quite this splendid, we look around to see how other people construct their homes and their lives—assuming that they know what they're doing, even if we don't. It's like a schoolchild copying from someone else's test paper: She sacrifices her integrity and may get the wrong answer anyhow.

In reality, we all have within ourselves a blueprint for just the home that will shelter our spirit. This blueprint doesn't deal in design and dimensions; it is the plan for home as a spiritual construct, for that homey sense of safety and belonging that can come with us from house to house and from one phase of life to the next.

Home by this definition needn't be confined to a specific building or set of circumstances. It is less a location than an intention. This is an important concept to grasp: When one or two or several human beings inhabit a place, it takes on an added dimension. It is still a brick house or a two-bedroom condo, but it is also someone's home. On the physical level, when a building is left to its own devices the natural principle of entropy, gradual decay, takes over. When people live there, this can be reversed; the structure can be preserved, altered, improved upon. In a more subtle way, people put energy into a place, an energy that can be felt and identified. When this energy is warm and welcoming, you can't help but want to pull up a chair and stay a while, whether you're sitting in your own living room or visiting someone else's.

The desire for this kind of environment is pervasive. Manufacturers of furniture and household fixtures count on it to sell their products, and decorating magazines depend on it to sell subscriptions. When we move from one place to another, we expect to find this ambience in the new residence, or bring it with us.

In addition, most of us have some mental image of the "perfect" home and its inhabitants. When this ideal is truly our own, a faithful replica of our inner blueprint, it gives us something to strive for in creating and maintaining homes that both serve and express us best. In many cases, however, too much of our model comes from outside ourselves, from society and media, and we end up with a prepackaged image, a sort of clip art archetype that most real-life homes have no chance of matching. My adopted image of home and family was the generic model, including two parents, two kids, a white picket fence, and a Border collie in the weed-free front yard. It's picturesque, but I don't live there. To favor the fantasy over my actual home was to sell short both my home and the life I live in it.

The happiness of home is not reserved for only one kind of person, one type of family, or one time of life, as the vignettes at the end of this chapter attest. The people in these households live different lifestyles and see the world in different ways, but they all understand that home is not the sole province of architects and other professionals; it is, rather, a design of nature. Even wild animals construct homes for themselves. Making a home isn't a matter of passing muster and following someone else's rules. It is declaring who we are in the place that is ours to do it.

What is the ideal home in your imagination? Do you live in a home like that? Does anybody? If something in your actual home seems missing, what is it—a partner, a child, a house instead of an apartment, a big house instead of a small one? There's nothing wrong with wanting any of these, but between desire and fulfillment there may be days or years of living. If you believe that having a "real home" depends on someone or something you don't have, you deny yourself much of the joy available to you in the home you have today. Wherever it is and whoever, if anyone, shares it with you, you do have a real home, and the option of making it even more fulfilling.

I struggled a lot with the "real home" concept after my husband died when our daughter was four. The word "family" didn't seem to apply to just Rachael and me, even when I factored in the three cats. But in the Chinese language the word *jia* is used to mean both home and family: Every home is a family, and every family is a home—including those comprised of a single parent, single kid, and feline foundlings. I liked that notion better than feeling domestically disadvantaged.

Now my daughter is fourteen and we have a dog as well as cats. Our home is quite real and our family, although not traditional, is vital and viable. I work at home and Rachael does homeschooling. I write books; she writes music. In the past year, we've hosted a cat funeral in all seriousness, a dog wedding in all frivolity, and a memorable weekend with houseguests from Arkansas, Florida, and China all at once. This sense of "open house," this availability to friends and fun and inspiration, is how my home serves my spirit. This is how I thrive. Your demographics may be different, but your need to unearth joy from the specifics of life is the same. The necessity to know ourselves, express ourselves, have a base from which to go forth into the world, feel loved, and give love is shared.

Love is an amazing commodity; it spreads to fill the space available. Home can be a splendid site for the healing activity of love, but it is also the place where love can be generated for dispersion elsewhere. It starts with loving ourselves through attending to our needs, treating ourselves to some blissful indulgence every now and then, and acknowledging our divine essence every day. Love's healing activity spreads outward as we care for the place we live and for the plants, animals, and very special people who inhabit it with us. It can expand to encompass our neighborhood, community, and world, and at the same time help us stay focused on what is genuinely important.

So much of life deals with the externals of what we do for a living, what we produce, how we look, and what we own. Externals even intrude at home: having emerald green grass or unchipped china can, some days, seem really necessary. But when you set out to satisfy your inner self instead of some invisible panel of judges, you'll find yourself making a home in which the externals are quite pleasing, even though they're no longer your primary focus. Their value lies in how they depict who you are, and in how you feel when you're around them. When you operate from the assumption that home is indeed a spiritual entity, mundane activities, from purchasing a pot holder to hanging a picture, will at times be inexplicably delightful.

This concept of home as a special, even sacred, place is not new—it's in our collective consciousness already. Many early religions featured deities who protected dwelling places. Followers of the European earth religions devised charms and spells to sanctify and protect their households. Similar rites exist today: the housewarming and the increasingly popular "house blessing." (You'll learn how to do one in chapter two.) In the Jewish tradition, after the destruction of the Temple in Jerusalem, regulations that formerly applied only to that rarefied center of divine presence were extended to the everyday world; and rabbis encouraged their followers to make holy places of their homes and godly statements of their lives. In China, Confucius taught that home, with its atmosphere of love and respect, should be the model for the world at large; and the Chinese mystical tradition of Taoism suggests that the body, the home, and the planet are similar organisms reflecting the Way of holiness, the Way of balance.

Holiness and balance don't necessarily come to mind when life is overflowing with demands and the sink is overflowing with dishes. But when you can strike a personal balance in the midst of these, you catch a glimmer that holiness is here, too. "In the mud and scum of things," wrote Emerson, "always, something sings." When your home is to your soul's liking, you'll find something to sing about more often.

Figuring out what a soul fancies is not difficult. Your soul wants what *you* want—not necessarily what you're supposed to want or what you've been told you want, but what touches you at your core. Maybe it's watching your child sleep, or digging in your flower beds, or renting classic movies on Saturday night. Whatever makes you think, "Life doesn't get any better than this," is food for your soul.

## A Soul Symposium

A technique for overcoming the obstacles that make these experiences less frequent than we'd like is the *soul symposium*. Its purpose is to help you get in touch with your inner self and create a richer, more contented home. Although there is certainly a time for family meetings, discussions with your roommate, and the like, this event is private. To conduct the symposium, sit down early in the day and lay your concerns on the table. Mentally put into words or write down any problems or situations you would take to an expert home management committee if you had one. The truth is, you do. It is comprised of your own inner wisdom, intuition, and good sense, working in peak form because you're committing this day to paying attention to them. You have within yourself already either the answer you're looking for or some direction on where to go for additional guidance. When you do a soul symposium, you temporarily stop trying to figure out what to do and instead allow existing solutions to surface.

Whatever is on your mind, bring it before your invisible committee and resolve to follow the two rules of a soul symposium: (1) Leave your concerns with the committee. Fretting over them and discussing them are not allowed today. You're welcome to worry again tomorrow, but for now put the problem or the decision you have to make out of your mind. Let the committee handle things.

(2) Expect useful insights and commit to noticing them when they nudge you. Your soul committee is not a strong-arm gang—its suggestions will come quietly and delicately. Promise yourself that for this one day, featherweight cues will be sufficient.

After doing this exercise one morning last year, I went to breakfast at my favorite bookstore coffee shop. One of the concerns I'd put on my soul's conference table was that our family dinners had become increasingly catch-as-catch-can, because of my daughter's early evening music and drama classes. Although I wasn't thinking about dinner as I ate my blueberry bagel, I did feel the urge to stop in the cookbook section on the way out of the store. Ordinarily, my logic would have jumped in with, "Cookbooks! Are you crazy? You don't have enough time to cook as it is—the last thing you need is another cookbook." But because I'd given my critical faculty the day off and was open instead to inklings from my soul committee, I went to that department and found a book called *The Fifteen-Minute Vegetarian Gourmet.* I bought it and that evening made a three-course supper of stuffed shells, French bread with pesto, and a maple-orange ambrosia—all in the promised fifteen minutes. Making a presentable meal in no time one night convinced me that I could do it other nights, and I have. (There will be more on giving dinner its due in chapter four.)

Finding that cookbook was a small thing. If you're struggling with some serious predicament, my example may seem trivial. Nevertheless, it is illustrative of how a soul symposium works. Whether you're dealing with a crisis or simply needing to choose between a good option and a better one, put the concern on the table and listen for your committee's recommendation. It is amazing how dependably the right people, information, and ideas present themselves when you allow your committee—your own wisdom, intuition, and common sense—to work unhindered.

Certainly a soul symposium can focus on some aspect of your life other than home, and you can hold an informal one on short notice any time you need it. *Just remember that those things that get attention flourish.* If you want your home to make you happy, make it the topic of a symposium every once in a while—and show it respect, admiration, and gratitude the rest of the time.

## Staking Claim

This is your *home*, whether you own it, rent it, or were born into it. Home is where you go to refuel—physically, emotionally, and spiritually. You no more need to own the house for this personal refueling than you need to own the service station to get gas. When your soul claims an address as its own, it doesn't matter if you stay there six months or the rest of your life. While you occupy the space, it is undeniably yours.

Sometimes it is difficult to feel really at home in a place you don't think you'll stay at long. People keep cherished objects stashed away until they buy a house, or buy the next house, the better one. But this is your home today, even if it isn't where you plan to be ten years from now. For some, the obvious impermanence of renting may be disconcerting, but in reality, everything is impermanent. According to Buddhist teachings, we can only know peace after we understand that impermanence is the very nature of life on earth. When we accept that nothing lasts forever, we don't have to frantically hold on, fighting change like Don Quixote battled windmills.

No one has absolute security in a house or in a life. Lease-free renters are said to live month to month, yet we all live just moment to moment by a genuinely amazing Grace that deals in hope, promise, and synchronicity. We need a place to consciously connect with this Grace as surely as a carpenter needs a shop or an artist needs a studio. We can worship in a church or temple or mosque. We can go away on retreat. We can tour the world's sacred sites. But the lion's share of our personal and spiritual growth takes place at home. It happens in the midst of the telephone ringing and the teakettle whistling and a student selling magazine subscriptions who is knocking on the door. It happens both in spite of the distractions and because of them. Away on retreat, it's easy to be lofty. Hanging on to your halo some Monday morning when the car won't start is another matter.

Someone asked noted psychic Edgar Cayce, "Am I growing spiritually?" Cayce's reply was, "Ask your family." Home offers unparalleled opportunities for growth. It is amazing how seldom our polished public persona even makes it through the front door. At home, degrees and titles and vitae don't mean a thing. Home deals with basics: whipping up something to eat, finding your keys, turning from what you're doing to listen to someone who needs to talk. These basics boil down to three realities of home that, once assimilated, make its sheltering of your spirit a matter of course:

*Home reality #1:* There are always things to do. My grandmother used to say, "A man must work from sun to sun, but a woman's work is never done." What used to be a woman's work is still never done. It's just that now everybody is supposed to do it.

*Home reality #2:* Somebody always needs something. When I got up this morning, the dog needed to be let out, the cats needed to be fed, my daughter needed a ride to her art class, and my neighbor needed a jump-start. That's how it is at home. If I were staying at a hotel, I wouldn't have to do anything except open the door for room service.

*Home reality #3:* Home is life in its most fundamental distillation. Seemingly humdrum occupations like making your bed in the morning and checking the doors at night link you with the passage of time and the rhythms of humanity. The rituals that surround waking and sleeping, as well as those related to eating, washing, worship, and family life, bear striking similarities wherever on earth you find them. These homespun habits are as human as having an opposing thumb. Although they are routinely disregarded, they deserve to be honored.

We live in a place and time when it takes courage and determination to give home priority status, or even realize that it might be a good idea to do so. Most of us are gone a lot, and when we do come home, we're often tired—weary from a variety of activities and torn by conflicting commitments. Sometimes we actually seek these activities out because they don't ask as much of us as the demands at home. Besides, achievement in the outer world is often accompanied by a level of fanfare that domestic accomplishments seldom receive.

Even so, there are pioneers among us who are engaged in a sort of homesteading of the heart. These are young people who are redefining home for themselves after experiencing a familial environment that was frightening or belittling. They include moms and dads who sacrifice the extras so one parent can be available for the kids, and divorced couples who make creative custody agreements that give their children not only the love of two parents, but the security of one primary home. They are adults in midlife who find the strength, patience, and resources to care for aged parents at home, where elders can make a contribution and remain an important part of the family. These pioneers include all the people who are making day-to-day, domestic choices based on loving convictions.

Although the call for a simpler, more heart-centered and home-centered way of living is coming from both religious and secular pulpits, it is the people who are transforming their own lives, in their own homes, in their own ways, who are quietly and unobtrusively changing the mores of our culture. Their diversity confirms that there is no single way of relating to home and family that is right, making all other ways wrong. A home is a signature, distinct and recognizable. Out of available circumstances, and often in spite of them, a warm, welcoming home can grow. The love put into it may be the greatest accomplishment of a lifetime. Those who believe there is nothing beyond this life say that the love we give here is all we really leave behind. Those who believe we go from this world to another say that this love is all we take. Either way, it forms the foundation of a home, as solid as stone and as deep as memory.

## The Shelter of Retreat

*Toni and John and their daughter, Lindsay, moved to the Midwest from southern California. They live in a fifties ranch house on a suburban side street. Their neighbors are other industrious young couples, lots of children, and pets. "Unless you're lost or know exactly where you're going, you don't end up on our street," says Toni, a personal trainer and fitness instructor at an upscale health club. John manages restaurants.*

*Although their house is usually filled with Lindsay's friends—plus three cats, a dog, and a surprisingly endearing rat—it is for the adults a hideaway, a retreat. John is analytical and has set aside a room for his computer, his books, and the data he needs for his rotisserie baseball league. Toni is artistic and has christened the guest room her creative space.*

*"My home gives me my self-esteem," she says. "I work at keeping it up and keeping it beautiful. I'm proud of it. That doesn't mean it's always perfect. Summer is disruptive—too much heat and too much activity. But in the fall there is order, in winter there is tradition, and in spring there is growth. Spring is when I'm needed by my rose bushes and the grass and the flowers. I renew my house and it renews me."*

## The Shelter of Individuality

*Necia is a divorced woman of forty-four whose rambling, Arts and Crafts–period house is a three-block walk from her massage therapy practice. Living and working in the same neighborhood make her protective of her "urban village," where she keeps an eye on the neighborhood children and a finger in local politics.*

*Home is Necia's prime expression of her individuality. "In order to manage in the world and be in business with the public," she says, "you have to sometimes put on another face. But at home, I live the life I want to live. I am particular about who comes in here. I get to pick the people who become part of our extended family. I get to pick the food and the smells."*

*Necia and her teenage son, Jamal, live in one part of the house; the other is a private apartment for her mother, offering a comfortable blend of closeness and autonomy. Because all three play instruments and sing, the house is often filled with musician friends playing jazz, blues, and the classics. Other times Necia cozies up in her oversize bed with a favorite TV show or music from her stereo, giving back to herself after a day at work giving to others.*

*"My house is a manifestation of my soul. The soul is ethereal; you can't grasp it. But when I walk through my front door, it's like walking into my soul. I like myself and trust myself. In the same way, I like my house and I can trust it to be a safe place."*

## The Shelter of Family

*Jan and Bill live on eighty rural acres. They built their house themselves, work in a home business manufacturing wooden toys, and cultivate a substantial garden. Gardening and toy-making keep them busy in the warm months, but winter is devoted to homeschooling their daughters and cultivating personal interests.*

*During recent winters, Bill built a family-size hot tub, restored a vintage cabin cruiser, and enlarged their house— doing everything himself, including plumbing, wiring, tile work, doors, and windows. Jan's winter activities include playing early colonial music with friends and making beaded jewelry as a side business.*

*"The family is our central focus," says Jan. "My life centers around the children. When our eighteen-year-old left to study in Europe last summer, I saw clearly how spending time with her had paid off. She bought the ticket herself, got through customs, and took trains and buses on her own—all in Italian. She is capable and confident. That's what we're working toward with all the kids. That's where I get my greatest satisfaction."*

## The Shelter of History

*Suzanne is a fabric artist with grown children and an inimitable sense of style. While visiting a friend, she spotted the apartment she knew would be hers a year before making the geographic relocation necessary to claim it. Once the curtains were up and she had taken her first bath in the big, deep tub with ball and claw feet, Suzanne was at home in the charming second-floor walk-up.*

*She staked out the neighborhood as her own, taking walks in the morning and getting to know the people in her building: the silver-haired ladies on the first floor who inspired her to deck her balcony with flowering plants, and the Vietnamese couple and their baby who live across the hall.*

*After a few months, she rented a second flat in the building, a basement studio, as her workplace. "When I walked down the old wooden stairs, it meant something to me that my feet fit exactly in the worn spots where women over the years have walked, carrying their laundry."*

*There is a sign in front of Suzanne's building stating, "FORMER OWNER HARRY TRUMAN." A historic notation is right for the place she lives, because her spirit thrives on a sense of history. "I'm so bonded with the urban flow of life, with the presence of older structures. I want to take responsibility to maintain the integrity of what has been given us by the carpenters and craftsmen. It is important for me to cooperate with those who have gone before."*

# The Shelter of Sustainability

*Mary and Terry married four years ago in the Mennonite church. Her two children from a previous marriage live with them much of the time. After having gotten to know the area by renting nearby, they bought their house for a good price—frugality is an important value for them. Within weeks, the house started to take on a new character: a tree swing went up in the front yard, a tree house in the back, a terraced organic garden on the side.*

*Their environmental conscience is evident everywhere: clothes drying on the line outside, an attic fan for summer cooling, recycling of everything imaginable. Mary, an environmental engineer, is currently on sabbatical, learning what home has to teach her. Terry took a turn at this as well. Now he is back at his job as an environmental designer, commuting via bus and fold-up bike.*

*"Our home gives us boundless opportunities to live out our environmental ethic," Mary explains. "It isn't always easy. Right now, for instance, we're battling Bermuda grass and I'd love to go out and buy herbicide. But it's gratifying to think that the way we live may be making a small difference, and to see some of it rubbing off on our kids."*

## The Shelter of Community

*Ellen is a young single woman, a book editor in New York. Her apartment is tiny but filled with meaning. She cleverly uses the dining room furniture inherited from her grandmother throughout the flat: the glass hutch is in her bedroom housing sweaters; the small credenza is her nightstand; the bigger one is in the living room holding her stereo. She buys fresh flowers every week and uses them as a centerpiece on her grandmother's sizable table that just fits in a corner of the living room. "I don't use the furniture as it was intended, but it's my grandmother's things that give this place its sense of soul."*

*She collects thrift shop heirlooms, too, like the hand-embroidered cotton runner that covers the top of the bookcase. "That runner means the bookcase won't have to be painted. I know myself and I'm not handy that way. I wouldn't love my apartment if I thought I had to do a lot of painting and fixing."*

*Ellen is handy with people, though. She uses her high school Spanish to converse with the super. "I'm the only one who does that. He lights up when he sees me." She talks to people in the elevator every day, too, finding out who they are and what they do, creating community by taking the initiative to do it.*

*When an adjacent apartment became vacant, she arranged for her best friend to get to see it first. "Now that Holly lives next door, there's a wonderful, cozy feeling here. In this big, anonymous city, there's someone I can visit without putting shoes on."*

## The Shelter of Beauty

*Greg Tamblyn is on the road half the time, singing in concert his songs like "Clyde, My Inner Guide" and "The Shoot-out at the I'm OK, You're OK Corral." Home, when he is there, has to be a place to work and a place to get away from work. Having a peaceful refuge to recuperate from traveling, a quiet spot for songwriting, and a gracious space for entertaining are equally essential. "There are a lot of aspects to my personality," he says. "I need a home where I can be different people."*

*He has found it in a roomy carriage house on five city acres. "I come home and discover new places to read or write or meditate. This year I have a garden. It's really secluded, and digging in the earth there is very restoring." His outgoing side is partial to the sunny kitchen with its antique fixtures and has a penchant for drawing guests like a magnet. The kitchen is the one room he never uses for writing, thereby honoring the kinds of creativity the room itself engenders—cooking and conversation.*

*With limited time at home, Greg has learned to eliminate the demands that don't carry a high priority. Renting this carriage house, for instance, frees him from the maintenance chores that took him away from his composing when he was a homeowner. "It's supposed to be the best thing you can do financially to buy your own home," he says, "but I've been so lucky to find a place this wonderful, this amazing, that if I tried to buy something even close it would cost four or five times as much. I can invest money other ways. I live here because it's good for my psyche."*

## The Shelter of Commitment

*Gladys marked her ninety-third birthday last year. Five generations of family members celebrated at the residence where she's lived for forty-one years. Since moving into the stone house on Chestnut Street, her husband passed away, she retired from her job as a community coordinator, and she witnessed two decades of "white flight" from the neighborhood. "People were always calling to ask if our house was for sale and I said no, that we bought this house to stay all our lives. I have always worked for the cause of integrated living. If I sold, I would feel I was betraying what I'd worked for all these years."*

*She lives with her son, Bruce, and she gives him the credit for her staying in her own home long after most people would have moved to a retirement center. Bruce cares for the yard and does the bulk of the housework. "There are things I'd like to do to my house," Gladys says, "but if they're beyond my physical strength, I don't worry about them." She still does the daily cooking, however, and the dusting, and helps with the dishes.*

*For twenty years after her retirement, the spare bedroom upstairs housed a lending library specializing in books on personal and spiritual growth. Hundreds of people came through her tidy quarters to borrow books and discuss religion, science, and philosophy. In those days, she had a special place for meditation, but she takes a freer view of such things now. "I meditate when and where I feel like it; it's not something rote anymore. Besides, I think our whole house has a peaceful feeling."*

# 2
# Making a Home

Sixth, seventh, and eighth grade.
Every Thursday afternoon it happened and every Thursday afternoon I detested it: homemaking class. It was just for girls then.
The boys were in shop using dangerous power tools. But we got to
serve them the bizarre dishes we cooked—like that tuna-pea
casserole with the potato chip crust. Then we had to sew the
checkered gingham apron decorated in cross-stitch, the equally
checkered gathered skirt that could somehow double my width
instantaneously, and the glazed-cotton blouse that may yet exist in
some landfill, the front and back panels still not joined.

Homemaking class missed the point for me because it concentrated on skirts and casseroles—the same pattern, the same
recipe. It effaced the individuality—the peculiarity even—that's
necessary to bring a home to life. My favorite house other than my
own was that of my classmate Becky. She, like me, was a child of
divorce, and as far as I knew, she never saw her dad. Nevertheless,
because she lived with her mother and her grandparents and had a
great-grandmother down the block, Becky's house seemed to have
love mixed in with the paint and varnish.

The house itself was far from perfect when appraised by the matching furniture and olive appliance standards of the day, but I thought it was beautiful. There were crocheted doilies on the tables and lemon drops in carnival glass bowls. Becky's grandmother grew red and white tulips and served dinner on blue-and-white plates. We drank our milk from jam jars and whenever Becky's grandfather told his familiar stories, we pretended we'd never heard them before. The eccentricities were part of the appeal of Becky's house, and part of the welcome.

My homemaking teacher didn't have much patience with eccentricity, much less appreciation of it. Her class never intimated that even an imperfect home can be a magical place, and that making a home—truly making a home—is a soul-sustaining enterprise that no duly informed person would want to miss. Although I suspected as much then, I know now for certain that bringing this magical quality of home into being has little to do with gender, being married or not, having a houseful of children, or living with a piano and a cat. It has to do with recognizing this special place as our spiritual center.

While few of us nowadays lament our lack of casserole-baking abilities, too many of us have accepted that in this age of designer showcase houses, *Architectural Digest*, and emulation of the rich and famous, we don't have what it takes to make a home. But when you can defy the subliminal suggestion that newer or more expensive is better, you can create a home that is uniquely indicative of your personality and belief system, a home that energizes, enriches, and delights you.

My daughter and I were living in just such a place when the idea for this book started taking root. We were renting the ground floor of a duplex in Kansas City. The dining room had a built-in hutch and a bay window that let in great streams of light. Other than those features, on the surface at least, there was not a great deal to recommend it. Rachael's bedroom was too small and mine had a view of a brick wall. When the couple upstairs played music, we heard the words. And that bright dining room had to double as my office, so even "formal" dinners were held in the company of a computer, a photocopier, and a typically cluttered desk.

In spite of its shortcomings, we adored the place. I didn't pay much attention to the space constraints. I was always inviting people over, and they always came. There were children in the neighborhood and Rachael enjoyed two splendid summers of Rollerblades and lemonade stands. The local businesses included a half dozen ethnic restaurants, a bookstore, a crafts gallery, a dry cleaner's, a couple of vintage clothing shops, and the hardware store that has stood on that corner since 1913.

We fell in love with this community, and I decided that I wanted a piece of this neighborhood that was really mine. I wanted to buy a house, so I went to a real estate seminar to learn how to do it. The convener said, "When you shop for a house, leave your emotions on the curb. Have in mind all the things you want; expect to get seventy-five percent of them, and make an offer."

So I did. I lumped together everything I wanted in a house. My list had things on it like hardwood floors, two bathrooms, a fireplace, a garage, a fenced yard, a room for a proper office, and lots of light. What I didn't realize was that while some of those items were preferences, others were needs of my soul.

List in hand, I found a well-cared-for, three-bedroom house that had eighty-five years of character development and seventy-five percent of the things I wanted. It lacked a couple of my prefer-

ences—there was only one bathroom, for instance—but preferences can be done without or postponed. I bought the house. After
we moved in, however, I realized that something that had looked
like a minor disadvantage was actually a major one. The first floor
doesn't get a lot of light, and light-absorbing oak trim and chair
railing exacerbate the darkness. I wasn't conscious of it at the time
I bought the house, but having a lot of natural light is, for me, a
soul-deep essential. I don't just prefer it; I require it.

I'd made a serious error in judgment. I had expected that this
house would shelter my spirit until I was old and gray. Once I realized what I'd done, I knew I wouldn't stay here much beyond
middle-aged and tinted. In leaving my emotions on the curb and
downplaying my heart's desires, I made the biggest purchase of my
life based on borrowed priorities. In other words, I settled.
Everybody knows that in terms of the physical structure of a
house, it is critical to look for the settling that can indicate foundation problems with expensive solutions. It hadn't dawned on me
that the kind of settling I did could result in consequences equally
grave.

Knowing this, I will shop for a house again one of these days
and be wiser when I do. In the meantime, I've had to find avenues
for bringing this house more closely in tune with my soul's needs
because, unlike preferences, soul needs cannot be ignored.
Having mistaken one for the other in my home-buying adventure
has at least taught me how to recognize the difference between the
two.

One way to discern what your soul values is to mentally
explore your current home environment with paper and pencil
nearby. This is a practical exercise for anyone. It can be a godsend
when you're thinking of renovating or moving, and can provide

valuable insights as to the dwelling needs of your inner self, whether you are happy or dissatisfied with where and how you live now. To do this, list on one page the objects and qualities of your physical environment that you would like to change. On another sheet, list every quality you really like about the place as it is. Then sit quietly with your lists in front of you and consider every item. Jot down next to each one on the first page *why* you want it. For each notation on the second page, write *why* you like it. A simple word or phrase will do: "pretty," "comfortable," "saves time," "reminds me of trip to Mexico," "makes life easier," "sentimental value," "good investment," whatever comes to mind.

When you come to an entry that requires more than cursory labeling, think about what need this serves in your life (or what need it would serve if it is something you don't have now). If this is something you want, how do you feel that lacking it impacts your life? If it's something you already have, how would your life change without it? If, for example, you feel particularly moved by the thought of the pine tree on your property and the little room you've made into a personal study, you are probably dealing with soul needs—in this case, a need for contact with the natural world and a need for solitude. Soul needs don't have to sound so lofty, though; if your CD player or your treadmill comes up as a soul need, accept that it is one.

Should you find yourself amid surroundings that deprive your spirit of something it craves, correct the situation if you can. If you can't, love it the way it is for now. This is possible because there are two kinds of love: There is the immediate attraction, and the kind that grows on you. In dealing with my house's dark first floor, I knew immediate attraction wasn't an option, but I had a chance with grows-on-you love. With it, the object of affection doesn't have to change; you just come to see the person—or in this case, the place—differently.

## A New Way of Seeing

Seeing is a surprisingly subjective activity. We're physiologically equipped for visual registry of shapes and depth and color, but our interpretation of these raw data is psychological. Case in point: People who wear rhinestone-studded bowling shirts and decorate with dusty plastic foliage and souvenir snow-globes think their things are great. To them, it's our stuff that's tacky.

I once did a magazine interview with a local actress of whom everyone in town was in awe. She was tall and willowy with a porcelain complexion and hair the color of a chestnut pony. Her voice was as rich as hot fudge on French vanilla, and she talked about Ibsen and Chekhov and Tennessee Williams with such familiarity you would think they had just been over for cappuccino. In the midst of our conversation in her airy condo overlooking the city, she said, "You know, I'm not really beautiful." I was shocked. Of course she was beautiful. Everybody knew that.

"Look," she continued, leaning across the glossy mahogany table until her face was only a dozen inches from mine, "I actually have very plain features." At such close range, I could see that her eyes weren't enormous and her nose may have been a wee bit crooked, but I would never have thought so had I not been handed an invitation to scrutinize it. "I realized when I was quite young," she said, "that my life would be better if I were beautiful, so I decided I would be. That's the impression I've given ever since."

Just as she decided to be beautiful, you can decide to love your house or apartment the way it is right now. This doesn't mean you can never change it: that actress may have had a nose job by now, and I may have the wood in my living room patched and primed and painted glossy white. Until the changes happen, though, deciding to see a place differently and loving it the way it is gives you a veritable transfusion of positive energy.

Among the changes you can expect when you decide to see your surroundings with love are:

*You will speak about your home in a positive way.* This is pivotal. When people used to ask me how I liked my house, I'd say, "Well, it really doesn't get enough light and the buildings are too close on either side and there's this dark paneling. . . ." With that funereal recitation, I gave anyone who would listen instructions on precisely how to think poorly of my home and, subsequently, of me. I was ruining the house's reputation, the way it would sully a friend's reputation if I passed along disparaging gossip about her. So I quit.

I started to talk instead about the shiny floors and the easy way the rooms connect with each other. I talk about having breakfast on the front porch, and about the finished attic where I keep gift wrap in a big box that makes me think of Christmas, and out-of-season clothes in a steamer trunk that makes me think of my grandmother. I go on about my daughter's room, which is big enough for a six-girl sleep-over, and my office, which is so "exclusively used for business" I could hold an open house for the IRS. All these things that make me happy have been part of the house since the day we moved in. But only after seeing them from a new perspective did I begin to realize how much they add to my life.

A bonus that comes with speaking well of your home is that other people start to compliment it. Now that I've stopped bemoaning its deficiencies, I hear all the time, "I really love your house." And I can say "thank you" and mean it.

*When you decide to see your surroundings with love, you will "talk" positively to the structure itself.* When I open the shades in the morning, I thank the windows for being there—not aloud necessarily, but I remember to be grateful. When I make my bed, I think about how pleased I am with the room that is most clearly my own: the brass bed I bought with proceeds from my first big magazine article, the ceramic rabbit my daughter gave me for my birthday when she was in kindergarten, and the little altar I'll share with you in chapter seven. The more I acknowledge the things I like, the better I feel about everything else, too. This can happen for anybody. It's automatic.

*When you decide to see your surroundings with love, you will lovingly care for the place where you live.* We tend to think that we care for those we love, but we often come to love those we care for. We see this when foster parents adopt the child who has lived with them; or when a kindhearted soul feeds a stray dog and before you know it, it's not a stray anymore. This is behind the tale (a version of which is known to every realtor) of the family who fixes up a house to sell, and grows so fond of it during the sweat equity process that they never put it on the market. Caring for a place with love makes routine maintenance a little less routine and a lot more pleasant.

*When you decide to see your surroundings with love, you will start collecting memories here.* When you see the place you live in as warm and inviting, you'll want people to come over and share in the good feelings—even before you get a new dining room table. If you have children, or if you just know children, you can make your home a place for kids to congregate. The lively feeling left over should make up for the fingerprints and inevitable kitchen mishaps. Make private memories, too—reading, writing, gardening, doing craft projects, being alone with your true love. It doesn't so much matter what you do, as long as you smile when you remember it.

All this begins the moment you decide to see what's around you in a different way. Replacing the khaki wallpaper you've always despised might actually get done, or you may find yourself developing an uncanny appreciation for muddy green. Either way, regarding the place that shelters you in a positive light is the first step in befriending a dwelling.

As for me, I cherish my house today. This started when I began to look at it with love and appreciation. Time did the rest: celebrating holidays and adopting a dog and returning from travels to a house that welcomed us. With time we got to know our neighbors, had out-of-town guests, and saw the flowers come up a second spring. People came for lunch and dinner and parties and just to talk. Each one left something behind: some humor, some affection, some understanding. The house incorporated those intangibles the way a stew takes on flavors from a bouquet garni. Like the poet said, "It takes a heap o' livin' in a house t' make it home."

You can increase your home's soul-nurturing potential by spicing your interiors with books and art and memorabilia that reflect who you are. Your personal satisfactions will draw visitors back, too, because something your soul genuinely delights in will strike a chord with theirs as well. Tastes vary, but authenticity is universally appealing.

Some people have a native talent for creating comfort in their surroundings. They are the natural nesters. My friend Kevin is one of them. Every piece of furniture, every vase, rug, and candle in his house fits in exactly with its colleagues, because every piece of furniture, every vase, rug, and candle looks like Kevin. Every item in every room he serendipitously discovered or carefully sought. Nothing was "just picked up" or settled for. Kevin is consummately at home in his home, and that safe, sheltered feeling is contagious. My soul is as fond of an hour in Kevin's living room petting his cat as it is of an hour by the ocean or in my favorite art museum.

Like Kevin, we can all christen our dwellings with evidence of our own habitation. It doesn't take a lot of money to achieve this. It does take trusting your instincts. Interior designer Alexandra Stoddard writes in her book, *Creating a Beautiful Home*: "Get in touch with that spirit inside you. . . . Unless your decorating style—the outer expression of who you are—is in harmony with your inner self, you won't feel the proper rhythm that is so essential to all aesthetic compositions. Remember, style emerges when you accept yourself."

Our homes look best when they look like us, and they feel best when they feel like us. A sense of style is synonymous with self-expression. Your spirit probably couldn't care less about style in the conventional sense, but when you pay attention to your inner self and see that it is reflected in your home, you're liable to end up with a healthy dose of savoir faire anyway.

## A Home for the Senses

Your personal style is in good measure revealed by the sensuous dance of shape, color, sound, texture, fragrance, flavor, and growing things that surround you. Examine your house or apartment using all your senses.

**SIGHT:** Visually, does your home announce, "Brought to you in glorious living color" or "Life is varying shades of gray"? Carl Jung said, "Color expresses the main psychic functions of man." What colors make you feel like wrapping up in them? Are they represented frequently in your house and in your wardrobe? How can you put more of these shades into your world? Do you have draperies or tablecloths or large pieces of upholstered furniture in colors you truly dislike? If so, how can you phase them out?

And what about the play of light in your rooms? Light may not be a soul need for you as it is for me, but do register for yourself where you get natural light and at what time of day. How can you use electric lights, kerosene lamps, and candles to enhance your environment? Would painting a room draw more light in? (White is the most reflective color, followed by pale yellow.) Where in your home do you want brightness and where would you prefer warmth?

What visual impression does your home give overall? Is it cozy or cluttered? Open or barren? Are there bits of beauty to fascinate the eye? What shapes appeal to you? What features and objects in your home satisfy your geometric partialities? Do the things around you work well together? And the most important question: Do you like what you see?

**HEARING:** What sounds and what level of sound are pleasing to you? This is an individual call. For every person who relishes stillness, there is another who can't fall asleep without the hum of traffic.

Tour your house with your ears as the primary sense organ. What do you hear? Is the television usually on? How do you feel about having it in the background? Do you hear quiet that you appreciate or more quiet than you'd like? Do you hear city sounds—cars, voices, sirens, drills? Do these exhilarate or annoy you? Are you regularly subject to noises you consider unpleasant? What can you do to diminish or eliminate them? What do you hear of the symphony of nature: wind, rain, ocean waves or a flowing stream, the songs of birds, frogs, or crickets? If these are absent and you miss them, can you replicate them with audiotapes or discs, or a small indoor fountain to provide the soothing sound of moving water?

And how about music? "After silence," wrote Aldous Huxley, "that which comes nearest to expressing the inexpressible is music." Where can you hear it in your home? How often do you give yourself the gift of music that really moves you? One day last winter I was driving on mundane errands when Beethoven's "Ode to Joy" filled my car and my consciousness. It was just a minute of the piece to advertise an upcoming concert. My car does not have a fancy sound system. In fact, it doesn't have a sound system. It has a radio. But that was enough. One minute of the right music turned my day around.

TOUCH: This is our most primal sense. We began to forget how to use it as toddlers, every time we were told, "Don't touch," and we didn't. Today, do touch. Go through your house and touch the walls, the woodwork, and the objects around you. If there is someone nearby to help keep you upright, do this exercise with your eyes closed. Touch with your fingers and the backs of your hands and the sides of your face. How would your house "look" to someone without sight? How do you feel about it in a tactile way? How does your furniture feel when you sit in it? Does it support your back? Are the fabrics smooth or scratchy? Are there pillows to reach for when you want one? Is there a hassock for putting your feet up? Do you genuinely enjoy how your bed feels, or do you prefer the futon in the guest room or your kids' waterbeds?

What do your floors feel like when you walk on them barefoot? How do the carpets feel, and the throw rugs, and the wood and tile and vinyl? Are many of the surfaces you touch soft and comfortable, or are nearly all of them hard and unyielding?

Do your feet and your fingers find your home interesting or dull? Make a mental note of what they tell you.

SMELL: Compared to our fellow mammals, we can scarcely smell at all, and some research suggests that our visually top-heavy lifestyles are causing us to forfeit what olfactory ability we do have. The scientists involved in these studies suggest that we need to *practice* smelling. To do this, they say we should be conscious of smells and clearly communicate that to our brains, saying, "This is bread baking . . . This is lily of the valley . . . This is tempera paint . . . This is potting soil."

Even though the human sense of smell is not terribly acute, it is powerful. When friends of mine put their house on the market, their realtor told them to put a little pan of cinnamon, sugar, and water in a slow oven before prospective buyers came to call. She said that the aroma would send a subliminal message: "This is a warm, comfortable home. Wouldn't you like to live here?" (The house, by the way, sold in six days.)

Scent is intimately tied with our memory faculty. The summers after my sophomore and junior years of high school, my friend

Tina and I took French lessons from Monsieur Selvey. We were convinced that he was the most sophisticated man on earth—or at least in Kansas City. In his entryway was a huge urn of dried eucalyptus. To this day, every time I catch a whiff of eucalyptus, it reminds me to review a little *vocabulaire*.

What does your house say to your nose? Does it smell clean? Is it a fresh clean or a chemical smell? Have you opened the windows lately to let some outside air waft in? What aromatic elements have you added to your environment? Are your cooking smells heavenly ones like baked apples and gingerbread, or are they the type that keep the manufacturers of exhaust fans in business? What delicate essences are there for the sensitive nose to delight in? Consider a vase of carnations or a vanilla candle; shelf paper with a hint of rose, a cedar block in a closet, or spicy potpourri in a terra-cotta bowl. The scent of dried lavender sewn into a pillow lasts and lasts, and folklore contends that it promotes sweet dreams.

TASTE: When an infant is presented with an object, a sure way to learn more about it is to put it in her mouth. Although we are soon trained to rely far less on taste for information about the world, we never lose the enjoyment of satisfying this sense. Take a taste tour of your house. Start with the medicine cabinet. What do you think about your toothpaste and mouthwash? Do you really like how they taste, or are you just used to buying those brands? Is your dental floss flavored? Would you like it to be?

In the dining room and other guest-prone areas, are there baskets of fruit, bowls of nuts, or dishes of red-and-white peppermints or golden butterscotch discs? In your kitchen, is all the food kept hidden, or do you see ropes of garlic or hanging baskets of onions and potatoes? Are there clear jars or canisters holding beans and grains? When you browse through your cabinets and refrigerator, are you enticed by the foods you see? Do they appeal to your sense of taste and to your idea of treating your body well?

Is anything edible growing in or around your house? Are there pots of basil, oregano, parsley, and chives on a sunny windowsill? Are tiny alfalfa or mung bean sprouts germinating in jars on a counter? Do you have a vegetable garden or a fruit tree?

Complete the sensory circuit through your house by paying attention to a sense not confined to a body part but one that connects us with all that lives. I call it the *nature sense*. Ask yourself how much *life* is in your environment.

Numerous studies indicate that having companion animals enhances human health and longevity, that looking at fish in an aquarium calms the mind and lowers blood pressure, and having potted plants cleans the indoor air we breathe. According to NASA, aloe vera plants and fig trees can remove low concentrations of formaldehyde. Spider plants and philodendron can gobble up both formaldehyde and carbon monoxide (although philodendron is toxic to felines and not recommended for households with cats). English ivy likes benzene for dinner.

A while back, my friend Dolores splurged on flowers. Fresh out of graduate school with no solid job prospects, she was living in a house-sitting situation scheduled to last only four months. Nevertheless, she planted a wealth of geraniums and petunias and marigolds in the barrels and window boxes around the house. I thought of the Persian poem that says, "If you have two loaves of bread, sell one and buy a hyacinth, for it will feed your soul." Dolores gave her soul a banquet.

Even if it's only a single rose or a bunch of daisies, invite some life into your personal world before this day is over. It will bring with it an infusion of life for the entire household. The human spirit thrives on the elements of nature.

## Feng Shui 101

The ancient Chinese system of *feng shui* is one way to align the energies of rooms and buildings with those of nature. Pronounced "fung shway" and literally translated "wind, water," it grew from an agrarian people's realization of their dependence upon nature. It has been influenced through the centuries by the Taoist penchant for balance and the Buddhist insistence upon harmonious coexistence with all beings. Just as Chinese medicine holds that an unimpeded flow of life energy or *chi* is necessary for a healthy body, *feng shui* suggests that the free movement of *chi* through a structure results in a healthy building.

*Feng shui* can be a lifetime study. For our purposes, it is safe to say that *chi* travels best along curving paths. It prefers archways, ovals, circles, and octagons to sharp corners and harsh lines. It thrives on order; chaos disrupts the flow. Good *feng shui* is pleasing to the human psyche, and people whose homes and workplaces have it tend to feel good physically and emotionally. They increase their potential for creativity, prosperity, and loving relationships. When a place has poor *feng shui*, the converse is true. There are, however, purported "cures" for inharmonious architecture: a correctly placed mirror, crystal prism, set of wind chimes, plant, nature painting, or family photograph is said to deflect energy blockages and positively reroute *chi*.

When I first heard about *feng shui*, it sounded like a Far Eastern rendition of avoiding black cats and not walking under ladders. Anecdotes of its changing lives and fortunes seemed, well, anecdotal. Nevertheless, many of the principles are clearly in keeping with contemporary psychology. Cheerful people are healthier and more productive than glum ones, and a pleasing ambience in a home or office does contribute to happiness. The pragmatic brass of multinational corporations have consulted *feng shui* experts in the design of their Asian offices, and I found a student of the art to suggest some modifications for my American house. Although it could be written off to the placebo effect, I've liked being under my roof more ever since.

The following are some of the principles of *feng shui* as I learned them from my teacher, Shannon Bailey, and my favorite book on the subject, *Interior Design with Feng Shui*, by Sarah Rossbach.

*Correct placement of furniture:* To feel safe and comfortable in a room, it is good to be able to see anyone coming or going. For this reason, a working desk or favorite chair should be placed with a view of the entrance to the room. Traditionally, the bed is set diagonally across the room from the bedroom door.

*A large kitchen:* The belief is that a big kitchen is conducive to abundance, since the rich can afford plenty of food and need room for its preparation. In my small kitchen, I create the illusion of additional space with mirrors. An appropriate place for a mirror is where it can reflect the stove burners: Having lots of burners implies lots of food and, subsequently, an abundance of money.

*Cutting corners: Feng shui* practitioners believe that a corner jutting into a room is akin to a knife cutting into the human energy field. This can be corrected by hanging a prism or wind chime in front of the protruding corner. Square columns can be similarly problematic unless vines cover their corners, or mirrors, edges touching, are placed on all sides.

*Keep luck inside:* Good fortune stays in, says *feng shui,* when stairs do not lead directly to the front door. If they do, wind chimes between the stairs and the door are the remedy.

*Hearth sense:* Because it represents the natural element of fire, a fireplace is lucky, but furniture near or facing one is not. If there is no other option (or if, as I do, you *like* facing the fireplace), a mirror hung over it and plants on either side will encourage the movement of *chi.*

*Don't flush money away:* Although living where flush toilets are standard is a stroke of luck in its own right, *feng shui* warns against flushing cash flow (symbolized by water) from a home by a poorly placed toilet. It is considered unfortunate *feng shui* for the toilet to be the first thing seen upon entering the bathroom. If it cannot be concealed, a wind chime between it and the door will help.

*Harmony with nature:* If the home has a hill behind it, it is classically placed for perfect *feng shui.* Trees around a dwelling are auspicious, as is a nearby lake or pond. A circular drive or a curving walkway leading to the residence or apartment building is also an advantageous omen. (It goes without saying that anyone who can afford a house with a circular drive, wooded lot, and pond on the property has probably had some good fortune already.)

I have fun with *feng shui*—within limits, of course. For example, I moved the computer desk in my home office so I could see the door. To do that meant my view was, obviously, a door. Not bad, but not inspiring. So I turned my desk to face the second story window. It's at leaf level with a massive old tree where blue jays, cardinals, robins, sparrows, and doves vociferously congregate. I far prefer the amended view, *feng shui* or not. Of course, I did put a framed mirror on the desk. This way I can see the door and the robins, too.

## The House Blessing

Another way to increase the positive energies of your home is with a house blessing. One is often done for a new residence as a way to clarify your intentions for this place. Friends gather, usually the night before the move itself, to wish you well and imbue the waiting spaces with harmonious thoughts and loving feelings. But you can bless the place you've lived in twenty years just as easily as one you're about to move into. Consider having an annual blessing—spring cleaning for the atmosphere.

Invite people with whom you feel particularly in tune, friends whose qualities you would like to be reminded of when you enter your home. Ask each one to bring a prayer, poem, or ritual from his or her religious tradition or philosophical bent. Sit in a circle. (If you're doing this in an empty house, bring a few folding chairs for those who might have trouble sitting on the floor.) You and those you live with speak first, thanking everyone for coming and expressing your hopes for your new home. Then each person shares what he brought to read or do or say.

A house blessing is often concluded by ceremonially cleansing the environment with incense or bundles of sage, in the custom of some Native American tribes. With a lit stick of incense or a smoldering sage frond, each person goes through the house or apartment symbolically purifying it with the fragrant smoke.

Simultaneously, everyone visualizes negativity vacating and the potential for health, happiness, and abundance coming to life in every corner and crevice of the residence.

At the blessing for our house, people were having such a good time they decided to bless the front and back yards and the garage, too. I'm sure it gave my new neighbors something to talk about: "Incense in the yard! Who are these people?" But once I got to know the fellow next door and the families across the street, I disappointed them all with my ordinariness.

For pleasant feelings that linger, you might include in your ceremony a large pitcher of water placed in the center of your circle of seated guests. It symbolically catches the blessings as they are offered. As the water evaporates, it diffuses them into the air. Our pitcher of aquatic blessings stayed on the mantle for nearly a month. Every time I glanced at it during those unsettling weeks of moving in, I thought of the people who had taken time from their lives to put some love into mine. In those moments I agreed completely with Emily Dickinson: "My friends are my estate."

## Everyday Magnificence

Obviously, a house blessing is not a substitute for an alarm system and good locks. The best *feng shui* on earth won't bring harmony to an impossible relationship or prosperity to a spendthrift. The beauty of these practices, though, is that they are simple actions you can take to increase your awareness of everyday magnificence. You don't have to wait until you build your dream house in the Rockies to put life and color into your home. It doesn't take a penthouse in Manhattan for your surroundings to reveal your uniqueness. Having the home you live in right now is really quite a wonder. The original miracle, of course, is simply being in a body—the soul's mobile home. The miracle compounds when you consider that elements from the earth can provide shelter for you while you're here.

When I become overly concerned with my own goings-on, I sometimes remember to go out at night and look at the stars. Even a celestially abbreviated city sky helps me put things in perspective. I seem smaller and, subsequently, the circumstances of my life that take so much of my energy seem smaller, too. When I look at the stars, the fact that there is at least one planet with life on it and a place for me helps me feel appropriately awestruck.

On this amazing blue ball, you have a place to be. You have somewhere to stretch out your body and your mind, rearrange the furniture or rearrange your thoughts, learn to get along with the most important people in your world, and get to know yourself intimately. In the enormity of space and time that culminates in here and now, being in such a place is truly remarkable.

I realize we don't spend a lot of time gazing at stars and marveling at the cosmos. We're more likely to see the stack of dirty dishes on the counter, the stack of bills on the desk, and the kids' room where the mess isn't even in stacks. It's enough to make you want to go back to work where the environment is controlled and you only have to do your specific job, rather than take charge of a domestic nation.

But in the landscape of our lives, making a home is front and center. The consensus of every major religion—and the majority of people who consider themselves happy—is that the primary task of human beings is to learn how to love. We can learn that at the grocery store and in the boardroom and on a bus to Pittsburgh. At home, with pretenses hung in the closet next to the business suits, we learn it best.

# 3
# Simplifying

I love to go to Susan's house. There's space between the furniture. You can see the wood floors. At Christmas she can put up a tree without rearranging her living room. There are empty places on the bookshelves for more books. There is room in her house for gifts and guests and possibilities. That's because Susan knows how to simplify.

Maybe she was born with the capacity to cull the inconsequential from the basic. Perhaps her mother had it, too, and her grandmother, and they passed it down, like a recipe or a figure of speech. But those of us who didn't grow up with a knack for simplifying can learn how to do it later in life. We have to learn how, in fact, if we want a home and a life that nurture our spirit.

Cluttered rooms and complicated schedules interfere with our ability to treasure the moment. Ironically, our houses and apartments—where some of our best moments can be—seem to attract clutter and complication like a magnet. Mail, both the welcome and the unsolicited, is delivered; purchases are unloaded; items accumulate. After several years spent in one place, it can feel as if moving would take more effort than climbing Mount Everest.

And think of the hours in the day. Are they packed so tightly they make your basement and garage look orderly by comparison? That's true for most of us. We fill hours like children of the Great Depression fill pantries: to the brim—just in case. The things the majority of people find the least time for are exercise, healthy meals, meditation, time with their spouses and children, and pursuing their dreams. Some couples even have to book appointments for making love. It's not an extra sitcom there isn't time for; it's the indispensables that are dispensed with.

You may be familiar with the sense of uneasiness, even desperation, that can accompany a growing awareness of how much "stuff" is pressing down on you. There are various stopgap responses to it: a garage sale to deal with object overload, a weekend away as a break from incessant responsibilities. But with the proceeds from the sale we shop again, and when we get back from our trip there's more to do than ever.

The only sure way out of the miasma of excess is to embrace simplicity, although our cultural ambivalence toward the concept can get in the way. Sometimes we like simplicity. We say, "These are great directions—really simple," and "Her dress was simple and elegant." Other times we're not so sure. "Simple living" can conjure up visions of voluntary poverty, subsistence farming, and sixties dropouts. To clear away some of the confusion, let's examine simplicity, first by looking at what it is not.

*Simplicity is not poverty and lack:* If you've experienced those, you know that juggling bills and chasing checks don't simplify anybody's life.

*Simplicity is not self-denial:* It is an indulgence, providing you with a wealth of time and space.

*Simplicity is not going back to the land:* Unless that's your chosen way to live and you know what you're in for, you'll end up with more complications than you ever dreamed of in Cleveland.

*Simplicity is not boring:* Contrary to popular belief, the alternative to incessant activity and acquisition is not vast emptiness. Instead it means experiencing life more fully than ever.

*Simplicity is not giving up what you need:* It is having everything you need with the bonus of being able to find it.

Now, what simplicity is:

*Simplicity is discerning the essential from the unessential:* Even with a commitment to living simply, you'll have lots of possessions and pastimes that aren't essential to your survival or your spiritual well-being. You just won't mistake these extras for necessities.

*Simplicity is having room for the unexpected:* In a simplified life, an unforeseen challenge—or a sudden blessing—can be incorporated without a lot of shifting and upset.

*Simplicity is savoring life:* It is having a truly memorable lunch with a friend because you didn't try to cram in breakfast with another one that morning as well as tea with a third in the afternoon. It's being charmed by the ceramic bowl on your kitchen table every time you see it, rather than having so many ceramic bowls that you no longer notice any of them.

*Most of all, simplicity is freedom:* It's freedom to choose what you want in your life because you're not letting in everything that shows up. It's freedom to do what you want because you're not already committed to more obligations than you can handle and the maintenance of more objects than you'll ever use.

## Simplicity Customized

Simplifying ought to be simple, but since we live in a society built around complexity, it isn't. Therefore, expect some trial and error.

For example, my friend Clare joined a cooperative food-buying club. Twenty other families were involved, and the food they ordered was delivered to a central drop-off point once a month. Clare figured that by joining she would save money and liberate herself from her weekly trek to the supermarket.

It was a reasonable idea, but in every delivery period she had to attend two meetings and do three hours of co-op work. She found herself buying items she hadn't planned on to help fill minimum order requirements for other members. That lessened the amount of money she saved. And since she couldn't buy a month's worth of produce at a time, she found herself in the grocery store checkout line every seven days anyway.

She saw this happening early on, but it took her six months to quit. Why? Because belonging to a co-op *sounds* simple, and for lots of people it is. For Clare, however, this reputation for simplicity carried more weight than her own experience with its complexity—until her experience amounted to twelve meetings and thirty hours of dividing gallons of honey and peanut butter into sticky quarts.

Clare's misguided quest for simplification only affected her food shopping. Mine affected my whole way of life. After two years as a single mother, I became tempted by the myth of our culture that city living is complicated and country living is simple. So I moved myself and my then six-year-old daughter to the country.

Mind you, the most rural place I'd ever lived was a Chicago suburb. Even there my apartment was a block from the train station so I could get into the city in forty-seven minutes on the local, thirty-two on the express. My skills for living were city skills. I knew how to get cheap theater tickets, hail a taxi, install a dead bolt. Nevertheless, I was certain life would be simpler if we vacated our urban flat for a rented cabin in the central Missouri Ozarks.

A few days after we moved in, a teenage girl from down the road came to call. Or maybe she came to scare this city slicker out of her wits. Either way, she greeted me with, "If you find a snake under your porch and it's poisonous, you got to kill it." Oh. I asked how I was supposed to do that. "You got to kill it," she said earnestly, "with a hoe." I wasn't about to tell her that the closest I'd ever come to a hoe was a picture of one under "h" in my daughter's alphabet book.

In spite of my vast ignorance of country life, I did recognize that our winding road was one of extraordinary beauty. Nearby was a brook that actually babbled, and it flowed into a quiet arm of the Lake of the Ozarks. Around us rose the foothills of ancient mountains that once dwarfed the Himalayas. Did I love it? Did I meditate on its splendor all day long? Not exactly. More often I was asking: "How did I get myself in this godforsaken hellhole?"

I had hoped for simplicity, but moving to the country wasn't my simplicity. It was somebody else's. Because I was out of my element, I was forever driving my car into town, or to a bigger town. After living in the Ozarks nineteen months, my odometer matured by 31,000 miles.

My work suffered, too. Uninspired, I artificially forced myself into production with caffeine. I was always either jittery or exhausted. The most efficient way to send anything by Federal Express was to flag down the truck on Highway 5 at 4 P.M. I remember standing in the little photocopy shop one day waiting for the proprietor to finish a detailed explanation of his cousin's gall bladder surgery while he laboriously made copies of my on-deadline article one painstaking page at a time.

I finally said, "Look, I've really got to meet the FedEx truck at four." He looked at the school clock hanging above the copier. "Well," he said, rubbing his chin and contemplating the state of affairs, "I reckon you missed it." And I reckoned at that moment that I had missed the point on simplicity.

Someone who did get the point and shared it splendidly was Peace Pilgrim, a remarkable woman who walked more than 100,000 miles from the 1950s until her death in 1981, carrying the message that world peace must begin with inner peace. Her life was the essence of simplicity. She owned only what she carried in the pockets of her navy blue tunic—a toothbrush, comb, writing materials, and stamps. She walked until given shelter, fasted until given food. She encouraged those who heard her formal lectures or who met her along the road to simplify their lives as well. "Unnecessary possessions are unnecessary burdens. If you have them, you have to take care of them."

Peace Pilgrim never asked that anyone emulate her life, but she encouraged those she spoke with to bring their lives from the level of want to the level of need. Although she lived cheerfully without a home in the usual sense and found that she personally didn't need much else either, she also recognized that most people not only need a place to live, but also feel the pull of careers, close associations with others, and the accoutrements of family life. Our simplicity has to suit our individual personalities and our circumstances.

But anyone can start by knowing this: If you want more simplicity in your world, bring more simplicity to your home. This doesn't have to mean radically changing the way you live; in fact, as in my case, sometimes that only adds complications. In our homes, sometimes even the smallest alterations can greatly improve our quality of life. And once you're comfortable simplifying your home environment and the time you spend there, you'll be able to do some simplifying at work, in the organizations you belong to, and in the larger community.

There are probably hundreds of ways to decrease the complexity of anyone's domestic domain. To keep things truly simple, though, I'll stick with five time-tested ways to simplify your space and ten others to do the same for your time.

## Five Surefire Ways to Simplify Your Space

### *Pay cash*

I'm intrigued by the phrase "personal effects." It seems that it ought to mean the effect a person has on the world, but instead it means someone's belongings, acquired paraphernalia that hasn't yet gone to the junkyard. Curiously, some of the world's most effective people have had the fewest personal effects. Mahatma Gandhi's possessions at the time of his death are said to have consisted of his clothing—dhoti and sandals—his glasses, and a copy of the Bible and the Bahagavad Gita. Obviously, Gandhi didn't shop much.

Most of us, however, shop a great deal. We shop in malls and cute little boutiques and at the stands in airports and subway stations and hospitals. We buy things from street vendors and schoolchildren and tag sales. We find things to purchase through mail-order catalogs, classified ads, and cable TV. We shop for entertainment. We shop for therapy. And we shop more than ever before in the history of humanity because—for the first time in the history of humanity—we can buy almost anything with no money and nothing to barter. We can shop on a plastic promise, and all the glittering objects offered to us are as good as free.

Now I'm not opposed to shopping. I like it, in fact. And I like it more since I chopped up nearly all my credit cards. I did. Right down the middle and again through that corner that said "expiration date." Since then, I have sought to live by the principle of, by and large, only spending money I have. A hundred years ago, that was common sense. Today it seems wildly radical.

What has happened since I stopped shopping with money I didn't have is that my life has simplified on every level. I realized the magnitude of taking this step just a few days after I did it. It was dinnertime and a woman selling season tickets to the symphony called. I wanted to be nice—I've had jobs calling people when they were eating dinner and I know that anyone doing it deserves compassion. I didn't know right there between the broccoli and the rice pilaf, though, if I wanted a season ticket or not, so I said, "Thanks for thinking of me, but I don't have a credit card. Can you send me information in the mail?"

She was dumbfounded. None of the usual make-a-sale lines she had been taught were appropriate. There was no use in saying, "We take all major credit cards," or even, "If you don't want the full season, how about our convenient half-season?" Without my being rude or curt, I had freed myself from a twenty-minute sales pitch. When you're not using credit, people just don't try to sell you as much. That alone makes life simpler.

Operating on a pay-up-front basis, I rarely make impulse purchases and therefore don't acquire a lot of intensive-care items: bric-a-brac that demand polishing, clothes that demand dry cleaning. I am released from the culturally entrenched notion that anything I admire I should buy, and anything cheap that I remotely admire I must buy. Now I buy what I need and I buy what I love. And my house is looking more like Susan's.

Remember how good it felt when you were a kid and bought a toy or a present for Mom with your very own money? That's how it feels to pay cash, because you *are* shopping with your very own money. And you'll have more of it because there will be fewer bills to dog you. A questioner once asked Peace Pilgrim how she could stand to be "so poor." She replied, "But I'm not poor: I have my health, the sun in the morning, the birds singing—and even financially I'm richer than you, because I have no debts."

You may well want to use plastic for tickets, travel, phone orders, class registrations, and the like. A bank debit card is ideal in those instances. It looks like a MasterCard or Visa, and it works in ATM machines and for making purchases just like a credit card. The difference is, what you spend is immediately subtracted from your checking account. You get no bill and—like Peace Pilgrim—no debts.

However you wish to conduct your personal financial dealings, making even a minimal effort to charge less and pay cash more can guarantee you the following:

You will end up with less junk you wish you'd never bought, and your environment will be less cluttered.

You will look better in your clothes and feel better in your house because everything that goes on your body or in your rooms you will absolutely adore.

With fewer bills, you'll have additional discretionary income, and the satisfaction of being more fully in charge of your financial life.

Your expenses will be easier to keep track of, and because cash is so tangible, money itself will become more meaningful.

When you buy something you truly want—especially something you've "saved up for"—you'll feel like a million bucks. And you'll greatly improve your chances for *having* a million bucks since you won't be shelling out a fortune in interest every month.

### *Insist on Quality*

I have a crocheted vest that I bought when I was eighteen and worked at a specialty store over the holidays. The vest seemed expensive at the time, but it was skillfully crafted of good yarn. In the many years that have passed since I was eighteen, I've sent innumerable garments to rummage sales, charity, and the rag bag. I still wear that vest, though, and it is still beautiful. Quality is never outdated.

When you're thinking of adding something new to your wardrobe or to your environment, let quality be the keynote. Quality does not necessarily mean cost, and it certainly doesn't mean the current status value of a particular item. It means only allowing into your cherished space those things that either serve a useful purpose or bring you genuine pleasure.

The highest quality objects in my home are those made by my daughter. Her artwork, needlework, clay creations, and poems are more valuable to me than a wall full of Rembrandts. Next in quality are the heirlooms—and I don't have many—that connect me with other important people in my life or my heritage. For example, I have a quilt my great-grandmother made. It is folded on top of our piano—fitting because the quilter raised two daughters by selling Steinways after she was widowed in 1910.

Also high on the quality scale for me are memorabilia of my own life and travels, books signed by their authors, gifts from people I like being reminded of, and items that by their shape or texture or color make me glad they're in my everyday world. Only you know what denotes quality to you. In general, an object made by hand touches the soul in a way something mass-produced cannot. Items whose quality is determined by their practicality can come from almost anywhere, but those whose value derives from more subtle attributes are seldom found in big, barnlike discount stores. They're occasionally made of plastic, but not very often.

Look around the room where you're sitting. What things there meet the dual criteria for quality, in that they are both practical and aesthetically pleasing? Which ones have a definite purpose and are regularly used for that purpose? Which ones simply make you happy because they're in your field of vision? What else is in the room? The "what else" is what stands between you and the simplicity of space your spirit craves. Clothes you don't wear, books you don't read, little statues that don't do anything and you've never liked anyway make indirect demands that rob energy. You see them, but they don't reward your eyes. You have to shove them aside when you look for what you're really going to use. If you have too many of them, maintaining a sense of order will be impossible.

Test the contents of each room in your house or apartment with these two questions: "Is it serving a purpose?" and "Does it make me happy?" Remember, you only need a "yes" answer to one of them for the object at hand to be earning its keep. This querying can be the makings of a massive mental garage sale of "what else." You may wish to turn that into an actual garage sale or Goodwill donation. In any case, once you do this you'll know what is making your life richer and what is jeopardizing your divine right to simplicity.

Take those same questions with you when you shop. Envision your intended purchase in the place you've set aside for it. Will it be functional or genuinely promote happiness? If so, it's worth taking on. If not, you're sabotaging your simplicity. (If you can't decide, wait twenty-four hours. You can trust a decision made with some time behind it.)

When you aim for serviceability and quality and discard the rest, you will start to enjoy the simple act of *being* in your bedroom or your living room or your kitchen. People will begin to comment on how good they feel when they're in your house. They'll ask if you've hired an interior designer or a cleaning person. If you only lived in your house before, you're likely to start to love it.

### Do a Seasonal Closet Cleaning and Excess Purge

Paying cash and insisting on quality diminish the likelihood of accumulating simplicity-diminishing bunk, but it creeps up on all of us. Moreover, what is useful to us changes as our lives change. Ski gear is useful as long as you go skiing. If you break your leg and change your sport, it becomes excess. Sell it. Give it away.

Closet cleaning can be like sending your soul to a spa. As you discard the worn-out, the worthless, and the size 5 jeans that haven't fit in decades, you discard ways of thinking that no longer fit either. You don't have to belabor the point: "I am now cleaning my closet and my mind." Just clean your closet. Your mind will respond.

Don't feel bad if right now you don't even know what is in your closets. Just know that anything not useful or uplifting that is taking up closet space is taking up psychological space, too. Clean it out. Then you'll know what's in there. Approve of every item you keep and pass along the rest. Do every closet—not just the ones that hold clothes but those housing brooms, linens, tools, whatever. Do the same for drawers, the medicine chest, the refrigerator. An overview of your home is in order every season. Do the two-question test on each room and storage place and eliminate excess accordingly.

Once you've done the major eradication that starts the process, subsequent seasonal purges will be quick and easy. Remember: You're not giving up what adds to your life. Simplifying does not mean paring down to cold and stark. As long as what's on display or in storage serves you in any way, it can be a welcome part of your simplified lifestyle.

"But what about gifts?" people always want to know. "I may not like a gift, but I have to keep it." No, you don't. You may have to accept it. If you do, you have to say thank you. But once you've done that, a gift is yours to do with as you like, just as if you'd bought it yourself.

Several years ago, a friend brought me a large, wrapped package. As I tackled the paper and ribbons, she was saying, "I painted this when I was in art school, and I want you to have it because the woman looks so much like you." Wrappings aside, I looked at the proficiently executed oil on canvas. She was right. The model for the painting did bear a remarkable resemblance to me. There was a hitch, though. This was a painting of a nude. I had the decorating dilemma of the century: where to hang a nude that looked like me.

I thanked my friend and hung the painting in my bedroom so everyone who walked in the house wouldn't ask when I'd taken up nude modeling. However, carpet cleaners, window washers, and TV repairmen who did come into that room all said something like, "You look real nice in that painting." I'd say, "It's not me," and they'd say, "Well, it's real nice anyway" and chuckle. I appreciate my friend and respect her work, but I gave the painting to someone who doesn't look a thing like me.

When it comes to gifts, remember that anything given to you belongs to you. Treasure the giver, acknowledge the generosity, but don't compromise your simplicity. Sometimes we feel a responsibility to exhibit a gift should its donor drop by, but examine that sense of obligation: It could get you a houseful of sundry artifacts that don't make your life better. One option in dealing with them is to use your imagination: An awful scarf might make an interesting table runner, or a pitcher that clashes with all your glasses could be perfect for holding cut flowers. Another way to handle a gift that doesn't work is to summon your courage and call the Salvation Army.

"But what if the people who gave it ask what I did with it?" They probably won't, but if they do, you can say something like, "Your gift was so thoughtful, and since we weren't able to use it, we've given it to someone who can." If they expect more from you than that, they didn't give you a gift—they made you a trade.

When you exercise discernment about everything, accepted or purchased, that stays in your house, you will find yourself in the presence of something rare and wonderful: unsaturated space. This emptiness opens the door to those things that will enrich your life in new ways. What you want and need now is far more likely to make its way to you when you make a place for it. By eliminating the unnecessary, you create the void. Nature does her best to fill it. You decide with what and how much.

### End the Paper Chase

The mail is here. My simplicity is at stake. There are the weekly grocery ads that come unsolicited, the pizza delivery flyers, the catalogs from every mail-order company on earth as penance for having once ordered a set of sheets and pillowcases.

I carry the entire bundle to my desk. I put the envelopes in the recycling basket; the bills go in a file until bill-paying day. I take magazines to the breakfast room since I read them in the morning with my cereal and fruit. I read the letters last when I can spend time with them. If I'm in a hurry, I put them in a special basket and read them later. If someone has taken the time to write to me, I want to give that letter more attention than I give the light bill. Everything else I either tend to immediately, file, or toss for recycling.

One way to get less junk mail is to answer each piece with a postcard that says, "If I have ordered from you or contributed to your organization in the past, I appreciate that association. However, I wish to have my name immediately and permanently removed from your mailing list." (I had postcards printed with this message.) It also helps to put a note with every subscription, order, or contribution asking that your name not be passed on to other companies or organizations. And you can write to the Mail Preference Service, Direct Marketing Association, 11 West 42nd St., P.O. Box 3861, New York, NY 10163–3861, asking that your name not be sold to lists. But you'll need to write every year. Direct mailers are better than bloodhounds for finding and refinding any potential customer.

Become selective about the paper you allow into your space from other sources, too. I chose a day last week to accept all the paper offered to me just to see how much I'd get. The receipt from the veterinarian was a computer printout, 8½ x 11. The chiropractor had his newsletter ready and I took one of those. Two city council candidates were distributing handbills in front of the grocery store, so I stuffed them in the bag with the potatoes and celery— and the weekly community ad paper I picked up from a box by the door.

Then I had lunch with a friend who had written a children's story. "I'll read it and get it back to you," I said. "No, just keep it," she assured me. "I have plenty of copies." Fourteen more sheets—well, fourteen for the story, plus lunch and dinner carry-out menus from the restaurant. I quit after lunch. I was drowning in a sea of wood pulp.

We know our copious consumption of paper is environmentally reckless, but it has a personal price as well. All that paper goes into our homes and detracts from the beauty we should see there. Having to sort, read, and dispose of it takes away from the time we have to spend there. So deal with as little paper as necessary and set up a workable filing system for the rest.

A filing cabinet is a most useful piece of furniture. When I got mine, Frankie Grady, a self-confessed filing ace, helped me set up a very workable system. Here are her suggestions:

*Determine how you do paperwork: in one place, wherever it's sunny at the moment, whatever.* Use the equipment that suits your style: a stationery cabinet, a file on wheels, or minifiles you can carry.

*Use a container equipped for hanging files.* Inside each labeled, main compartment, use labeled file folders for each sub-category. The hanging files can cover broad, general headings like "house" or "finances," but avoid anything as all-inclusive as "miscellaneous." Example: hanging file—Car. File folders within that hanging file—Repair and maintenance; Insurance; Titles and Registration.

*Clear out a file or two every season, just like your rooms and your closets.* Be willing to part with unnecessary written and printed matter. The backs of used pages make fine scratch paper, fax-sending paper, kids' drawing paper.

*Put your important documents in a safe deposit box, and keep an updated list of what that box contains in your filing cabinet or computer.*

*If you have a computer, file as much as you can electronically.* Every once in a while clean out your hard drive, too. Excess is draining, even when it's bytesize.

### Organize—But Only After You've Simplified

Simplification and organization are often confused, but they're not the same. You could conceivably organize every bit of extraneous accumulation that's in your house right now. You could hang it on pegboards, stack it neatly on shelves and in cabinets, put it in drawers with those nifty little dividers, stick it on bulletin boards with matching pushpins, and place it by category in those see-through, stacking plastic boxes. In *Clutter's Last Stand*, Dan Aslett's classic on unfettered living, he calls most organizing aids "junk bunkers." If we didn't have so much junk, we wouldn't need all those places to keep it.

Be forewarned: If you organize before you simplify, things will be disorganized again in no time. This is not because you're a hopeless slob without a prayer for redemption. It is because *excess cannot be organized.* If it could, it wouldn't be excess.

Ask ten friends if they think they're organized or not. Unless everybody you know is a CPA, eight out of the ten will probably say they're dreadfully disorganized. It's a myth. We just think we're disorganized because we live in a time and place overflowing with junk.

If you practice the first four Surefire Ways to Simplify Your Space, you will find your environment becoming organized with minimal effort. When you remove from a desk drawer the broken rubber bands, dried-up pens, loose change, and year-old ATM receipts, what remains looks pretty good. So what if there's a paper clip in with the postage stamps? That drawer is, for all intents and purposes, organized.

You can organize further if you enjoy doing it, but it isn't necessary. Too much concern over tidiness and organization can defeat your purpose of making your home friendly to human beings, starting with yourself. We all have an internal clutter/order tolerance level. Some people need houses that look like Marine barracks when the sergeant is due in for inspection. Others aren't comfortable unless there are half-read books on the tables, an open sewing basket by the big chair, and last night's Scrabble board left out to summon another game this evening.

Find your tolerance point and compromise with the tolerance points of the people you live with and the conditions of your life. If you put the well-being of living things ahead of arranging objects, you will be somewhat less organized but quite a bit happier.

## The Time of Your Life

The other day I watched an attractive, professional-looking mother approaching a department store entrance at a trot, her little girl galloping behind her at two arms' length. The child was five, maybe six, one of those ages that only lasts a minute and never comes back. "Hurry up," the mother said several times. Her daughter tried to comply, while respecting the childhood conventions of studying cloud formations, running the fingers of her free hand along the turquoise railing, and of course not stepping on any cracks.

I was angry with the mother and I didn't even know her. Well, in one sense I didn't know her, but in another I knew her intimately: She's just me in a different phase of life. I said "Hurry up" to my daughter a thousand times and she obeyed implicitly. She hurried so well that she's a teenager now, and it took her no time at all.

Hurrying ourselves and those close to us is a harsher activity than we realize. We tend to be *short*-tempered when we are *short* on time. When we have the time to be patient, we usually are. When we have the time to listen, we usually do. When we have the time to help, we're glad to pitch in. Without the time, we feel pressured, flustered, and annoyed. We offer to be of service and then resent it. We're asked a question and we say, "What is it?" in a way that states clearly we don't really want to know.

As we add more activities to our to-do list, we become like a debtor adding creditors to the roll in an attempt to pacify those he already has. There is no bankruptcy court for people whose time account is chronically overdrawn, but you can recognize them. They're always racing. They can't sit back and enjoy themselves. They're terrified of "wasting time." They suffer from stress-related illnesses. Their relationships are strained. Their schedules are so full that even they don't know what's happening tomorrow. Misplacing a planner seems like losing a limb.

Too many physical objects to work around and care for can diminish our serenity, but too many obligations, too many activities, and too many hours at the office will wipe it out completely. We've heard Ben Franklin's phrase, "Time is money." In our era, time is better than money. The Americans' Use of Time Project done at the University of Maryland showed that forty-eight percent of Americans earning less than $20,000 a year would give up a day's pay every week for a day of free time. Seventy percent of those earning more than $30,000 a year would do the same thing. We crave more time and we're willing to pay for it. Of course, the richest person alive can't buy more than twenty-four hours a day. That used to be enough. Now, in spite of increased life expectancy and a bonanza of labor-saving apparatuses, the pace of life is more often than not a mad rush.

An occasional jam-packed day is exhilarating. As a steady diet, however, it weakens us physically—those adrenaline rushes tax the adrenal glands—and it impoverishes us spiritually. Thomas Merton said, "The rush and pressure of modern life are a form of its innate violence." We call a truce by simplifying our time.

This may be easier for you than clearing extraneous objects from your environment. For me, it's harder. A part of me likes the stimulation I can get from overscheduling and arriving where I'm going, out of breath, just in time. It feels like sliding into home plate with the crowd cheering. Of course, nobody is cheering, and when I collapse at home after an overly rushed day, I bring the agitation with me. Everything is here to soothe my soul—a delightful daughter, congenial pets, art and music hand-picked to suit myself—but I'm too tired, or too wired, to notice.

A couple of things had to take place to make me *want* to simplify my time. The first was that I saw my incessant busyness interfering with my closest relationships. The second was that serenity started to feel better than stimulation. It was like switching from strong coffee to herbal tea. At first it's wretched, but after a while it feels better to be naturally composed than artificially energized.

# Ten Surefire Ways to Simplify Your Time

### *Say No*

Just as you're saying no to gadgets you won't use and clothes you don't wear, you can say no to activities that aren't genuinely meaningful to you. Developing the habit of politely but consistently saying no when you want to will give you more time at home and more peace when you're there.

When something is important to other people, they assume it should be equally so to you. The art museum docents think you should be one. The neighborhood crime-watch people think you should drive patrol two hours a week. Everybody in the Save the Rain Forest group thinks you should carry a sign this Saturday. Maybe you should. And maybe not.

In Buddhism, there is a lovely concept called *dharma*. Roughly translated, it means "duty." But it means more than that. It implies an individual's special calling or purpose. When you feel fully committed to what you're about, you're probably doing your dharma. If you're lukewarm regarding it and proceed reluctantly, you probably aren't.

Our lives are multifaceted. We are workers, students, householders, lovers, parents, citizens, friends. All these identities can be part of our dharma, part of the tapestry of our destiny. Our task is to balance the many roles we play and refrain from volunteering to understudy everybody else's. It can be tough to say no, especially to causes we recognize as worthy. The goal is to realize that, since we can't help with everything, our time and stamina need to go into what truly speaks to our hearts.

## *Tithe Your Time*

Tithing money—donating one tenth of all income to a church, to people in need, or some other deserving cause—is a way of orderly giving. It not only enriches society, but those who do it believe that the practice blesses them with greater prosperity. (John D. Rockefeller's famous "Ledger A," on which he wrote his income and expenditures from boyhood, included a regular tithe.)

Time can be tithed also. You don't have to get specific—ten percent of waking hours—but you should be conscious of giving some time every week or month to something outside yourself. If lack of time is a problem, giving it away may not seem like a viable solution. Nevertheless, when you plan to spend a portion of the hours you're allotted in service to others, you will better organize those that are left.

Be sure you tithe your time to something that genuinely moves you, and say no without guilt to anything that doesn't. This way it will be easy to remember that you're giving a gift, not serving a sentence.

## *Put Things with Feelings First*

Balancing your checkbook is probably not as important as listening to your child. Having a romp with the dog should usually take precedence over waxing the kitchen floor. That's because bank accounts and linoleum can wait until a more convenient moment. Things with feelings can't.

Because the hours in the day are finite and many of them are already taken up with sleep, meals, working, bathing, and the like, it's crucial that our discretionary time be spent where it means the most. Put things with feelings first—including yourself.

### *Allow More Time*

Whatever it is you have to do, allow a little more time than you think it will take. That way, if it takes longer than you thought it would, you're covered. If it doesn't, you have some spare time, some breathing minutes. Leave for your appointment before you really need to. You won't have to drive so fast. If you get there early, you're not wasting time. Bring a book and read it. Bring your journal and write in it. Bring your spirit and meditate.

If you're expecting guests, plan for their arrival in advance of the appointed hour. That way you can rest before they're ringing your doorbell, and truly enjoy their visit once they get there.

### *Prioritize with the ABC Method*

Priorities change from day to day, which is why the ABC method of meeting them works so well. When you make your list of what you want to accomplish each day, label every item with a letter:

> *A*—priority; it must be done today
> *B*—important; it needs to be done soon
> *C*—necessary; it should be done sometime.

If you only get through your *A* list, you've done everything you have to. The following day, a *B* or two is likely to rise to *A* category. Eventually, even the *C*'s will be promoted—or they'll fade into insignificance.

### *Stay Well*

Nothing is more time-consuming than being sick. Days and weeks can be devoted to an illness, and more are eroded by having to use them to make up for lost time. If you are a hurrier, one way to get sick less· is to stop hurrying. Colds and the like tend to pounce on hurriers midrush. It's as if the body and mind conspire to force a rest on those who refuse to take one otherwise.

We can't always prevent coming down with something, but if we're aware of our state of health and take care of it on a consistent basis, we can substantially hedge our bets. How are you taking care of yourself right now? How is your nutrition? How much rest do you get? How regularly do you exercise? Are you frequently outside to get fresh air and a little sunlight? Do you meditate daily or have another routine for stress reduction? Have you sought out health care providers you trust and with whom you can communicate freely? The time you spend preserving your health is like time invested in a savings account; you'll get it back plus interest.

### Let the Machine Get It

Pavlov's dogs salivated at the sound of a bell, and we respond just as habitually: We answer the phone. We run in from the garden to answer the phone. We leap from the shower and track a rivulet as we dash in a towel to answer the phone. In the midst of a wonderful dinner, a romantic interlude, or the part in the bedtime story where the bears just walk in on Goldilocks, we say, "Just a minute," and answer the phone.

Alexander Graham Bell himself refused to have a phone in his study because he resented the interruption. If he were alive today, he would no doubt let his answering machine do what it was built for: answering the phone. If you are not used to letting it cover for you when you're home, at least part of the time, developing the habit can be agonizing. Every unanswered call seems like the sweepstakes people on the line to say you're suddenly rich. When no message is left, there is the nagging wonder: "Was it my long-lost love come back for me at last?" Of course not. Important callers leave messages. This was someone wanting to sell you aluminum siding, or a friend calling to chat who didn't leave a message since she was on her car phone.

Let the machine get it. Pick up the calls that are important, return the others at your convenience, and be grateful to the callers who didn't leave messages. They just gave you something precious: time.

### *Turn Off the TV*

Television can be educational, motivational, and uplifting. Families can watch quality programs together and discuss their meaning. Television can help us understand the world around us and people who are different from ourselves. Is that how you use TV? Me neither.

Regardless of what we choose from the televised menu, one thing is clear: Watching television takes time. The average American will spend *one year of life* just watching the commercials. If you want more time to enjoy your home, get to know your family, unleash your creativity, or ponder spiritual truths, turn off the TV. You may just want to turn it off from time to time and use that thirty or sixty minutes for something else. Or you may want to turn it off, unplug it, and give it away. Whatever choice you make, you and your television—and your VCR and your computer for that matter—have a relationship of which you are in charge. How much time do you choose to spend with electronic companionship? Spend that much and no more. This is your life, not a pilot for an upcoming series.

### *Put Off Procrastination*

My mother had lots of little "do it now" phrases: "Never put off until tomorrow what you can do today." "A stitch in time saves nine." "The early bird catches the worm." The early bird also doesn't have to come up with an excuse or pay a late fee.

If you look around your life and find a great many things undone, perhaps you're trying to do too great a number of things. Procrastination can be a problem for anyone, but it usually strikes lives by necessity. If you're attempting to do more than there is time to do, something has to be put off. And then something else. And another thing. Before long you're lamenting that you can't finish any of it.

If this is your situation, go back over the previous Surefire Ways to Simplify Your Time. Choose the one that you think would make the most difference in the time you have and do it for a week. That alone should give you the time you need to take care of your most pressing procrastinated issue.

An additional put-it-off problem arises when we misjudge what we need to do. We like some activities more than others and we tend to do those first, pushing the less desirable ones further into the abyss called "later." There are a couple of ways to deal with this. One is the jump-in method. That is, just jump in. Once a suspect task is begun, it's usually not so bad. Another device is to make something unpleasant seem less so. If you despise cleaning the bathroom, for instance, do it with the accompaniment of energizing music. Or bribe yourself with something luscious when you're finished—maybe a bath with scented bubbles in your bright, sparkling tub.

Procrastination itself is a time robber. It takes time to worry about a task, plan additional ways to put it off, talk about how awful it is, and feel guilty over not having done it. If you want more time and something needs doing, do it. Then you'll have time left over.

### Schedule in Fun

Even when time is a problem, most of us get our work done. We keep our houses reasonably clean. We care for our children. We take the car in for an oil change. We write to our parents and the friends who moved to Seattle, at least every once in a while. We do what we have to do. What we want to do, however, may never get done.

Right now put down this book and get out a pencil and piece of paper. Write down everything you want to do before you die. It doesn't have to be reasonable. Just write it. *Visit a pygmy tribe in central Africa.* Write it. *Locate my best friend from sixth grade.* Write it. *Learn to speak Icelandic.* (Why not? Lawrence of Arabia did.) Write it. When you catalog your heart's desires, it sets in motion a chain of events that is indeed uncanny. It's as if your sub-conscious reads the list and sets about to make it happen.

My daughter made such a list, a poster actually, when she was seven. It had things on it like, "Go to China," "Go to Paris," "Be in a movie." These seemed fantastic at the time—it was when we were living in the cabin in the Ozarks and sharing one closet. Amazingly, a surprising number of the events she entered have come to pass for her, including China, Paris, and the movie—even though it was a nonspeaking part in a low-budget horror flick.

We tend to downplay the importance of fun and of making our dreams come true, but these are our defenses against regret. Schedule in time for sheer pleasure, and keep your schedule flexi-ble to allow for impromptu delights. My plan today was to work on this chapter until it was finished. That's sensible for someone who writes for a living. But a neighbor called and said that everyone was meeting at the park for a picnic on this outlandishly warm winter day. I'm going, finished or not. My body needs fresh air and my soul can use some sun.

We were conditioned early in life to see work as more valuable than play, but play is the work of children. It is the finest way to learn, and it needs to continue throughout our lives. In school, we had courses that were "solids"—math, grammar, Latin, history—and "nonsolids"—art, music, poetry, sports. But what makes life worth living today, the fact that you can conjugate a verb, or that you can still recite Sara Teasdale and hit a pretty decent tennis serve.

Program your mind with this: Recreation is required. It is not optional. Look at the word: recreation. The time you give to it re-creates your soul. There's no waste in that.

## Bringing Simplicity Home

Eliminating the chaos from our drawers and from our days invites our spiritual self to make its presence known. In his book *Adventures in Simple Living*, Rich Heffern writes: "Cultivating a spirituality for simple living involves locating and exploring those places in our soul that ring like great jubilant wind chimes to the breezes and whispers of the divine. Simplicity . . . frees us from clutter so that we can wake up to and hear the great chiming within us."

Because "the great chiming" is inside us, it's available to us any time and any place. Chances are, though, we'll hear it at home. At home we're on our own time and in our own space—time and space we've cleared out to be amenable to chiming and such.

When the physical amenities of our homes are the necessary and the beautiful, just walking through a room can inspire us. When our calendars have substantial white space like a well-funded advertisement, we have more time to spend in this place where we can most thoroughly be ourselves. A simplified home feels friendlier. A simplified life seems easier. And remarkable joy comes from simple things—like having work to do that matters, and having people to love who matter a lot.

# 4
# Cooking

Preparing food and eating at home can be the most immediate way to touch home's spiritual essence. Food nourishes the body, home nourishes the soul, and when we avail ourselves of the two in tandem, we feel content and cared for on both levels.

In ancient Greece, Hestia, goddess of the hearth, was also the symbol of home itself. Her precedence over the place of cooking gave her dominion over the house as a whole. We still consider the kitchen the heart of the home. Whether we actually do much cooking or not, most of us like the *idea* of an inviting kitchen. Realtors attest that more often than not, the way potential buyers feel about the kitchen makes or breaks a sale, even if those buyers work elsewhere all day and eat out on the weekend.

In spite of the warm, homey images food can conjure up for us, we're living in the aftermath of a revolution that, in the second half of the twentieth century, turned agriculture into agribusiness and food processing into a major industry. These events took the source of food and a good part of its preparation away from the home. As a result, we are further removed than ever before from the plants and animals we eat. Most of the food consumed in America comes processed or packaged in some way. We think that reading labels makes us nutritionally savvy, yet the foods that the forty-two trillion cells of the body understand best are those that have no labels: the fresh foods direct from nature.

Taking the time to shop for and prepare these in our amply scheduled lives is no small challenge. With the full-time home-maker an endangered species, cooking is a job busy people attempt to fit in wherever they can. Although there is popular interest in entertaining and specialty cooking, many people find it difficult to embrace ordinary food preparation day to day. With so little time to cook, people use convenience foods. These are indeed convenient, but they rob cooking of its creative aspect. Without the creative reward, there is little incentive to cook at all, but since there isn't time to cook creatively, we reach for the convenience products again; and the cycle repeats itself.

We also eat out a lot. According to the National Restaurant Association, American men eat fifty-one percent of their meals at restaurants, American women forty-four percent. We eat out for business, pleasure, expedience, and the luxury of having someone else wash up. Some people also eat out because it is easier to let another person, even an unseen chef, nurture them than it is to nurture themselves. People who have made their homes their spiritual centers still go to restaurants, but when they do it's because they *want* to go to a restaurant, not because they can't face the prospect of washing a head of lettuce.

I can assess the quality of my spiritual life on a given day by my attitude toward preparing food. It's always easy for me to cook for guests: Their appreciation is ample payoff. Cooking for only my daughter and me is more of a challenge, and cooking for myself when she is away is a watershed proposition. Take a moment to reflect on how you feed yourself when you're by yourself. If you are not fully comfortable in preparing a lovely little solitary meal, try just once to serve yourself as you would serve a guest. Every time I do this, I can feel my self-esteem rise a notch and my quality of life follow suit.

A lot of people who I meet when I speak around the country, however, tell me that even cooking for a family can feel burdensome. Many are preparing food differently than their mothers and grandmothers did to bring their meals into line with current nutritional knowledge. This is a good move, but it can make food seem somehow less friendly than it used to. Others tell me that their life situation isn't conducive to cooking. Like single people who don't fancy cooking for one, parents tire of cooking for kids who complain about every entrée except pizza and pancakes. Differing work and school schedules make the image of gathering around the dinner table more fantasy than reality in many households; and in families with conflicting dietary needs and philosophies, the path of least resistance is often every eater for himself.

The facts are we know we ought to eat healthfully; most of our family circles don't resemble a rerun of *The Waltons*; and with the little time we've got, there's plenty to do besides cook. Underlying these facts, however, is a deeper truth: We feel ambivalent toward food preparation when we lose touch with the sanctity of food itself and with the truth that we can connect with the warmth and peacefulness of home through bean soup or pumpkin bread or potato knishes or tomato preserves—whatever foods suggest to us comfort and caring.

Without the fulfillment of these connections, people are more prone to "food issues"—chronic heartburn or food sensitivities or an obsession with chips or chocolate. Ancient writings from India teach that food itself has vibrational qualities that go beyond its tangible characteristics. The belief is that, in addition to vitamins, minerals, protein, and the like, food should give us life energy, what the yogis call *prana*. Fresh, natural foods have an abundance of this life energy, while stale, overprocessed, or highly chemicalized foods have very little.

In a subtle way, the state of mind of the cook can increase or decrease the amount of life energy in the food. The cliché "seasoned with love" may not be strictly metaphorical. It is part of Eastern wisdom that the cook's mental attitude affects a dish as surely as her liberality with the salt shaker, and this attitude has as much to do with a meal's effect on the eater as does its nutritional profile. When some character in an old movie says, "I'd sure like a home-cooked meal," he is voicing what many of us know instinctively, that eating food prepared by a caring human being and served in a congenial atmosphere is an enriching experience that's just not on the menu at the diner.

## Our Most Intimate Relationship

In a very literal sense, our most intimate relationship is with the food we eat. We participate with it in a biochemical alchemy in which the food becomes the cells of our bodies, subsequently affecting our health, our thinking, and ultimately our society. This makes cooking a lot more than "throwing something together." It's "putting somebody together"—or several somebodies, when you cook for a family or friends. Even preparing the simplest midweek breakfast or Saturday lunch has the purpose of sustaining the people who make up a home. This is a sacred act and a sacred trust. To come to realize this more fully:

Allow enough time for unhurried cooking and eating.

Learn to enjoy cooking.

Make your kitchen a room where you want to spend time.

Shop in places you'd go even if you didn't need groceries.

Acknowledge each meal with thanks.

Select the best foods for your body and spirit.

Share food with others, both in your home and from your home.

Let's explore each of these.

### *Allow Enough Time for Unhurried Cooking and Eating*

One dismal November, I was in Paris with a wretched case of the flu. Our little hotel had no room service so my traveling companions went out to get me something to eat. They were gone two hours, because none of the restaurants they approached had any concept of "carryout." There weren't any Styrofoam boxes and plastic forks. Finally, one compassionate restaurateur let my friends bring me dinner on the condition that they would return the china and silverware.

This is typical of the French, who take a decidedly enjoyable attitude toward meals, whether at home or away. In spite of their notoriously rich cuisine, they statistically compare to Americans as a little healthier and a lot trimmer. This is due, at least in part, to their respect for the art of cooking, a respect that translates into spending time with a meal—time that gives their brains the chance to tell their bodies they've had enough to eat. The French have also made an art of gracious presentation, dining amid lovely surroundings and good conversation.

It's often different here. In the fifties and sixties, there were drive-ins; it was a big attraction to eat without getting out of the car. Now there are drive-thrus for eating without even parking the car. To me, eating in a car is like making love in a car: It is cramped, messy, and you're unlikely to respect yourself in the morning.

If you can't sit and savor three meals a day, at least sit and savor one—in your own company or with people who matter, with the television off and the answering machine on. Having at least one relaxed meal each day is important for anyone and critical for children. Consider making one weekly dinner at home a really big deal. Dress for the occasion. Have hors d'oeuvres. Use the good dishes and linen napkins and don't eat, dine. Have guests on this enchanted evening if you like, but don't make the guests the reason for the evening. The evening is for you, your mate, your children, and your home.

If you live alone, don't always eat alone. Invite someone over for a cooperative supper: cook, eat, and clean up together. When you do cook and eat by yourself, make it a meditative experience. Focus on the food you're preparing and be in touch with the sustenance it's about to give you. Have a lovely place setting. Light a candle. Play some music. It may feel strange to treat yourself so lavishly, but remember who you are: a spiritual being having a human experience. You are certainly worthy of being queen or king of your castle.

**FAST FOOD:** Once speed-eating is addressed, we can look at our societal expectation that food ought to prepare itself in no time flat, thus the profusion of frozen entrées, ready-made meals in boxes and bags, and microwavable everything. I know that for many people, the microwave oven can make the difference between eating under their own roof or under somebody else's arches, so it certainly has a place. I personally don't use one, though. Aside from arguments about the safety of microwave ovens and opinions about the palatability of food prepared in them, they cook more quickly than our body-mind rhythms can keep up with. Because we take on something of the vibratory character of what we eat, I think microwaved food causes the gustatory equivalent of jet lag.

Certainly saving time is important. Hopefully, you have a little more of it as a result of using chapter three's time-saving techniques. There are other techniques that promote kitchen efficiency without robbing your experience of its creativity and civility. You might try, for example, fixing staple items like soup, rice, beans, or baked goods on the weekend to have for speedy warmups and brown bagging during the week. Favor quick-cooking foods like peas and tomatoes, which cook in five minutes, instead of Brussels sprouts and artichokes, which can take twenty to thirty minutes to cook.

Budget sufficient time for food preparation, but never overwhelm yourself with the chore. One complex item is enough for any meal. Serve it with a salad, a steamed vegetable, and fresh fruit for dessert. It's enough. It's healthy. It's realistic.

Also, rely on time-saving cooking methods like stir-frying, steaming, pressure-cooking, or using a simmer-while-you're-gone Crock-Pot. An Ayurvedic physician, one trained in the healing techniques of ancient India, suggested that I have my main meal at midday. Even though I work at home, I couldn't imagine taking off at 11 A.M. to cook, so I called into service the Crock-Pot I'd previously used only for heating mulled cider in December. The following morning I was greeted in the kitchen by the enticing aroma of lentils, onions, carrots, and spices that I had put in the slow cooker the night before. It was as if I had a maid or a mom who got up early to cook for me.

It also helps to have a repertoire of two or three meals that you can put together in a snap. One that I rely on is stir-fried vegetables—either over steamed rice (cooked easily in an electric rice cooker) or topping couscous, a fluffy wheat side dish that's ready in five minutes. Another immediate dinner is vegetable lo mein, using virtually instant fresh pasta or cellophane noodles. When I resort to leftovers, or when I use convenience foods, I still try to serve a little something that's freshly prepared. I either make a salad with nice Bibb lettuce or mixed baby greens, or I serve a loaf of today's bread from the neighborhood bakery. Its owners do the baking themselves on the premises. It isn't my soul that goes into the bread, but it's somebody's soul. In a pinch that's good enough.

### *Learn to Enjoy Cooking*

This is different from learning *how* to cook. Anyone who can read a recipe can cook. Learning to enjoy the process means discovering how to make it serve you as a way to unwind, to express yourself, and feel even more comfortable in your home environment. You can't force yourself to love cooking, but you can be open to the inner workings of getting food on the table.

Take a minute before you start to cook to bring yourself totally into the present moment and the task at hand. I learned from a Sikh friend to precede the preparation of every meal by putting my hands in prayer position to symbolically balance the polarities of light and dark, male and female, action and passivity that are part of all of us. She taught me then to offer a prayer that the food will be healing to the body and soul of everyone who partakes of it.

Whenever I remember to do this, I feel privileged to be the cook, instead of resenting having the job by default.

You can center yourself this way or by sitting quietly for a few minutes, taking a leisurely or energetic walk, or listening to music. What you do is up to you. Even the briefest time spent in some centering activity will ready you to experience each act of preparing a meal as something potentially interesting and pleasant. The feeling of water rushing over your hands as you wash spinach leaves, the softness of flour, the citrus spurt when you cut into an orange, the smell of garlic sautéing in a skillet or biscuits rising in the oven—these are glorious sensory experiences. Be aware of them. Add to the pleasure of the process by using the best equipment you can afford, pieces that feel good in your hand and that clean up easily.

Obviously, not every aspect of cooking is transcendental. Chopping onions and scrubbing pots are part of it. Even so, do what you can to avoid martyr-in-the-kitchen syndrome: "I'm tired of doing this . . . Nobody appreciates all I do . . . The hours I work, I should be able to hire a cook. . . ." Believe me, I've said all of these and thought of plenty others. They just never made me feel better. What does make a difference, though, is help in the kitchen. Cook with your spouse, your love, your roommate, your mother, your neighbor, your friend. And by all means, cook with your kids. Children adore cooking when they're little and if they start then, they'll be good at it by the time they can ride a two-wheeler. I think the reason children often cook surprisingly well is that they tend to be more interested in the process than in the product. They see this as a game and they're willing to try different versions. This attitude has no arbitrary age limits.

When my daughter was twelve, she became infatuated with

Middle Eastern food. She wanted to eat it more often than I was willing to take her out for it, so she learned to make it herself. She scoured our cookbooks for recipes and I bought the ingredients. The following evening she started on such an authentic repast that I thought for a minute I could see Mount Sinai out our kitchen window. About fifteen minutes into the act, she said, "I think there will be a lot of food. Maybe we should invite someone over." I made some calls but got a series of answering machines. I figured we'd have leftovers. But by the time she finished concocting the feast, we'd heard back from everyone I'd phoned and ended up with eight for dinner. The menu: Greek salad, stuffed grape leaves, *spanakopita* (spinach pie), and baklava for dessert. The guests left happy and some stayed to do the dishes.

Of course, nobody feels like making dinner every night and sometimes it's great to go out. Another perk of learning to enjoy cooking is that people who do often develop a sixth sense that lets them know when they've found a restaurant with a chef who really loves to cook. It goes beyond innovative dishes and pleasant presentation; it's more the sense of life energy these chefs' enthusiasm imparts to the food. You can almost taste it. When your meals at home have this life energy, you come to recognize and expect it.

### Make Your Kitchen a Room Where You Want to Spend Time

If you're going to create in your kitchen, the room needs to be as conducive to creativity as a painter's loft or a potter's shed. It doesn't have to be an architectural wonder with four sinks, an island, and state-of-the-art appliances in serious stainless steel. It should, however, be efficient, fit your lifestyle, and lift your spirits when you walk in.

The most important thing, I think, is that the kitchen stays neat. I can live with smudgy mirrors, undone laundry, and paw prints on the living room floor, but I need a reasonably clean kitchen. As long as the dishes are done and my shoes don't stick to jelly when I walk from the stove to the refrigerator, I am sufficiently at peace with my house to avoid being haunted by the *hausfrau* within.

If the general layout of your kitchen ranks high on the efficiency scale, both cooking and cleanup can be carried out easily. Generally speaking, an efficient kitchen is one that has plenty of counter space, the sink and appliances near each other, lighting that's adequate but not harsh, and storage that's ample and easy to reach. If this doesn't sound like your kitchen, there are less drastic ways than moving or remodeling to approach the ideal.

If counter space is at a premium, for instance, can the items that have staked a claim there go somewhere else? Do you use the blender, food processor, or electric can opener enough to warrant their taking up counter space all the time? Maybe they can go on a shelf or in a cabinet—or can you install a built-in shelf? Can you discover hidden work space—a pull-out cutting board hiding inside your cabinets or in the microwave cart, for instance? Does your kitchen table have a surface tough enough to work on? How about buying an inexpensive, over-the-sink cutting board? It can provide eighteen to thirty-six inches more space to chop and dice, mix and stir, and set things.

If you've done the simplifying procedures from chapter three, you've already increased your kitchen's relative storage capacity by putting to pasture underemployed gadgets. You can make for even more efficiency by rethinking arrangement. Are staple foods and regularly used items easy to get to? If there are children in the house, are their dishes and snacks where they can reach them? Can items used only occasionally—the picnic basket, the heart-shaped cake pan, the punch bowl—be stored in another part of your house or apartment? Is there an order, at least to you, in your kitchen?

Ideally, you should be able to open your cupboards and know that you're being helped, not hindered, in your task, whether it's pouring a glass of lemonade or preparing a five-course dinner. If that isn't the case, get one cupboard or one drawer at a time put together in an orderly, usable fashion. If you're not neat by nature—heaven knows, I'm not—it won't be perfect, but it will be better. The same goes for the refrigerator: Clear it out every week before you do your food shopping.

Beyond basic cleanliness and order, a welcoming kitchen says something about you. The most lasting way to imprint this personal signature on the room is to spend time there. If your kitchen is large enough to have a table or breakfast bar, conduct some life from there. Talk with your kids there when they come in for a snack. Talk with your mate there in the morning. Talk with friends there when they come by for coffee.

If your kitchen is small, make what memories you can in it with anybody who'll fit. If you cook with a buddy, you'll probably bump into each other a few times, but that's part of the charm. When my house was built ninety years ago, it had a big kitchen. Sometime between then and now, someone built a wall that added a room but cut the kitchen dimensions by two thirds. My wish list includes getting it restored to its original size, but for now I cook compactly. It's good training in keeping utensils washed as I use them, and being mindful of where things are and the space they're taking.

There is a framed photo hanging in my kitchen that reminds me that small is relative. It is a picture of Droma's kitchen. Droma is a friend of mine in Tibet. She lives with her husband and son in a two-and-a-half-room company apartment provided by the textile factory where she works. That "half room" is the kitchen. It is about the size of a hall closet—maybe three feet by four or a little less. In it is a primitive gas stove, one churn for butter and another for the traditional Tibetan yak butter tea, two buckets of water—one for cooking, one for washing—and stored foodstuffs. It was from this tiny space that, the last time we visited, she regaled her guests with *tsampa* (a traditional barley dish), three kinds of dumplings, cabbage, potatoes, and even *chang*, homemade barley beer. Having that snapshot on the wall somehow enlarges my kitchen and diminishes my greed.

Look around your kitchen. Is there something you can see that speaks to your deepest self like this photograph from a far-off land speaks to mine? This might be a little saying in calligraphy hung over your sink, your grandfather's cast-iron skillet on a rack over the stove, or art done by your children or grandchildren decking the refrigerator door. (Respect young artists by keeping this installation rotating so each work can actually be seen.)

Let edibles enhance the atmosphere, too. The Greek poet Homer called fruits and vegetables "gifts of heaven." Keep some out in the open to grace your kitchen with their bright colors and delicate fragrances. If you have enough sunlight, grow fresh herbs. Let your kitchen be a lively place. Its reason for being, after all, is to give you life.

### Shop in Places You'd Go Even If You Didn't Need Groceries

Today I bought my groceries at a store that insists on feeding my spirit even before I filch the first grape from the bunch in my basket. It is called City Garden. That's not a phony name either, like those housing developments called "Fox Crossing" or "Hare's Gate," when neither a fox nor a rabbit has been spotted there since 1947. City Garden really *has* a garden on a formerly vacant lot across the street. It supplies a goodly portion of their produce and makes a corner in the inner city bloom.

The store itself is a comely compilation of brick and hard wood, decorated for each season in fresh blossoms or dried flowers, gourds and pumpkins, or holly and evergreens. Its stock is basic natural food store inventory, invitingly displayed on antique shelving, with dry items like nuts and noodles bagged and placed in oak cabinets with glass-front drawers. The deli salads make an oasis of color—purple and orange and green. But in the bakery the only colors that matter are shades of brown: the color of Colombian coffee and chocolate chips, oat-raisin cookies and wheat-bran muffins.

Going to City Garden is a joy for me, like a walk in the morning or a good movie. Shopping at a supermarket is more like doing sit-ups or listening to pledge requests on PBS. The reality is, I have to buy the groceries. My response to that reality is that I insist upon having a good time doing it. The mood I take on at the store will come home with me. I don't want to bring agitation or ugliness into the place I work at keeping harmonious and beautiful.

Think about your neighborhood, your town, your city. Is there somewhere you can shop for food that makes you feel as glad to be there as City Garden makes me? It may be a surviving corner store, an outdoor farmer's market, a family-owned ethnic grocery, or a health food store that has barrels of brown rice and rye berries and gives free cups of herbal tea. Maybe you can't buy every edible you need at your favorite place, but can you get more there than you do now?

If supermarkets are the only food stores available to you, comparison shop for atmosphere the way you would for bargains. Even if you live in a small community with only one supermarket, you can make a point to shop when the friendliest checkout person is on duty, or when the just-baked rolls still scent the aisles, or on the day the produce arrives at its freshest and most attractive.

In any store, get to know the people who work there. When you are a familiar face with a name attached, your opinion matters and your concerns are taken more seriously. When you become more than an anonymous consumer, you begin to assert your personal power when it comes to the food you eat. There are a variety of ways to expand this take-charge attitude: Some people assiduously clip coupons; others grow a garden, take autumn jaunts to "pick-your-own" farms and orchards, or buy shares in a Community Supported Agriculture project.

A CSA is a small farm that sells shares of the upcoming season's produce to families and individuals. When you own a piece of the farm, you reap a portion of the harvest—bountiful bags of vegetables if the weather is good, a few straggly potatoes if nature has not cooperated. With most of us living in cities or suburbs and our children believing that food is manufactured at the supermarket, this vicarious farming provides a valuable education.

Another way to be more closely involved with the food that will furnish your cabinets is by joining a food co-op or buying club. Although it wasn't right for Clare, the woman in the last chapter who found belonging to a co-op too time-consuming, others thrive on being part of a group that orders cases of quality food products from a cooperative wholesale warehouse. Not only do they save money by eliminating the retail markup, but, more important, they meet in members' homes and share in the work and the provisions. This makes the co-op a sort of extended family. Storefront co-ops offer this kind of community on a larger scale. Members devote time to keep the operation going and are remunerated with deeply discounted purchases.

Wherever you choose to shop, remember that every time you bring a bag of groceries into your house or apartment, you are bringing something of the store in with them. How do you want your house to feel? Shop in places that feel that way, too.

### *Acknowledge Each Meal with Thanks*

Buying your food from a place you like and having a positive attitude while you cook bless your meals in a general way. To bless your food directly and personally, grace—spoken, sung, or in silence—works wonders. I have heard that people of high spiritual attunement can choose from an array of dishes which ones have had grace said over them. I don't claim to have that level of awareness, but I do make a point to say grace or sit in respectful silence before I eat. I brought into adulthood the table blessings I learned as a child, simple ones thanking God for the food. One day when Rachael was small, she came home from a friend's house with a mealtime prayer thanking the earth and the sun for their part in the process. So my prayers expanded, remembering the forces of nature, and the farmers and the truckers and the recipe creators.

I realized that even when I cooked for myself and ate alone, an unseen multitude converged at my table. And when I took a bit of silence for reflection and thanks, I was weaving a thread into the time-honored tapestry of human experience. "The act of blessing our food and giving thanks for our lives is as ancient as humanity,"

John Robbins wrote in *May All Be Fed.* "It is a profoundly spiritual act, and reminds us that we are not alone in our prayers."

I have a hunch that blessings compound. The fiftieth prayer of thanks said around your table is even more valuable than the fifth, because it's building on all those that went before. Routinely saying grace puts your entire house in a state of grace. You can taste it in the food and feel it all around you.

### Select the Best Foods for Your Body and Spirit

Pure, natural foods are as indispensable for spiritual development as for physical well-being. This is because the body, built by the food we consume, is the monitoring station for every impulse—physical, mental, emotional, and spiritual—that we receive or transmit.

A philosophy with a great deal to say about food is yoga. For health and spirituality, it recommends fruits, vegetables, whole grains, raw nuts, and fresh milk. These are believed to be calming in their effect, nourishing without exciting or depressing the nervous system; and their ease of digestion provides the body with nutrients without its laboring too hard to extract them. It is said that these foods are favored by persons seeking spiritual growth and inward bliss. When they predominate in the diet, people feel more peaceful within themselves and bring increased equanimity into their homes.

Although this diet was described centuries before cancer and coronary heart disease were documented, it comes astoundingly close to the one currently recommended for prevention, and in some cases reversal, of these diseases. This way of eating, low in fat and heavy on fresh fruits, vegetables, and whole grains, is also ideal for avoiding obesity and its complications.

For making a home a spiritual center and the kitchen the heart of that center, this way of eating offers even more. Think about it: Fruit is fast food par excellence, always ready to eat, no matter how little time is available. Crudités and lightly dressed salads can also be prepared quickly, and there's very little cleanup afterward. Fresh produce in season and whole grains and beans are the least costly items on anybody's grocery list, even without their bonus of built-in "health insurance." These foods tend to smell nice, entice the appetite without encouraging excess, and tempt the eye with their shapes and colors. "Dining is and always was," said architect Frank Lloyd Wright, "a great artistic opportunity."

Moreover, simple foods from nature are kind to the planet and its inhabitants. This is especially true of foods grown by organic methods. Before World War II, what we today call organic, people called food. Eating grains and produce grown without synthetic pesticides and herbicides is neither radical nor new, but chemical agriculture is.

In choosing organic, you avoid possible residues of synthetic chemicals in your family's food and in downstream waterways. You also support a style of farming that builds the level of organic matter in the soil, thereby enriching rather than depleting it. An organic farmer works in partnership with industrious earthworms and friendly microorganisms to keep the soil alive and vital, so the food it produces is alive and vital, too. It costs a little more at the checkout counter, but its benefits to our families and our planet are priceless.

A predominantly vegetarian diet extends these advantages. It's thrifty in terms of land, water, and energy consumption, so it can feed more people. And healthful vegetarian cuisine is rich in culinary potential. People used to think of meatless eating as doing without. Now it's seen more as making room for all the exotic vegetables and grains they've never tried before. In addition, many who avoid meat from an ethical standpoint feel that their homes are more benevolent spaces as a result.

This doesn't mean that only vegetarians have spirit-sheltering kitchens, or that you must revolutionize the way you eat to have such a kitchen yourself. For cooking and eating to do their share in making your home a haven, though, it is essential that your food choices be conscious ones. They need to be true choices, not habit patterns. Awareness of what and how we eat helps us choose foods that make us feel best, on every level of our being.

Swami Vivekananda, who in the nineteenth century was the first Indian spiritual teacher to travel widely in the West, once said, "Don't make your kitchen your church." It is possible to focus so intently on food that we get stuck there, like being held hostage in a grocery store. Be willing to make progress toward eating lighter, purer foods. Celebrate small changes. Listen to your body, and try to feed it what it needs.

### *Share Food with Others, Both in Your Home and from Your Home*

Deep satisfaction can come from sharing food with friends, acquaintances, the needy, even animals. When you share food *at* home, blessings abound within your walls. When you share food *from* home, the blessings find their way back. It's like the old story about the difference between heaven and hell. In hell, there is a beautiful banquet set out, but the people's arms are tied to spoons so long they cannot reach their mouths. Heaven looks just the same—banquet, four-foot spoons—but in heaven everyone is happy because they're feeding one another. For heaven on earth, then, feed people—literally and figuratively.

There used to be more of a custom of sharing food than there is now. I think this is because more people in earlier times raised their own food and it was what they had to give. "Neighbors bring food with death and flowers with sickness and little things in between," Harper Lee wrote of a 1930s Southern town in *To Kill a Mockingbird*. It would do us well to resurrect this practice of bringing food and flowers and little things, home to home, for all occasions and for no occasion at all.

When I returned home with that Parisian flu, still unable to venture far from bed, Mary brought fragrant miso soup with a splash of Chianti. Dody brought spicy vegetable soup in a Folger's coffee can. Susan brought potatoes and onions and carrots right into my kitchen, made creamy potato soup, and brought it up to me on a tray. I regained my strength on friends' soup and friends' caring.

There are myriad ways to share food, in your home and from your home. Making double batches when you're cooking something special means that you have extra to take to a neighbor, an elderly person, or overburdened friends. When someone you know is expecting a baby, start double-batching the month before her due date. This way, there will be a dozen homemade dinner items in her freezer for the family's adjustment-heavy early weeks with a newborn.

Potluck dinners, luncheons, and brunches are excellent for getting people together without overworking a host. This way, everybody shares food, and your home is blessed with camaraderie. A variation is the dinner co-op in which two to four families, couples, or individuals commit to making dinner for the others one night a week or one night a month. In some co-ops, everybody eats at the host family's house. In others, the people scheduled to cook pack up the dinners and deliver them to their co-members, who get the bartered equivalent of a catered feast. This is a rather unconventional way to procure dinner, but it's a simple idea that can be of real benefit to busy people.

Sharing food with the needy is a fulfilling experience as well, and doing this can offer valuable insights into oneself. It used to be that when there were food drives for the poor, I would shop especially for the drive, but I shopped differently than I would have otherwise. I bought what I thought "poor people" would like. Then I went through my own lean times. I liked the same foods I always had. Now when there is a food drive, I "shop" from my own cabinets. This shows me how much I have, and it is a clear reminder that those who need help are no different from me.

Assisting with the cooking or serving at a homeless shelter, a church, or a soup kitchen is another way to share. Although you probably won't be serving food from your own kitchen, you'll be sharing from your own giving spirit, and you'll bring the good feeling home. Helping is always good, but we tend to get absurdly seasonal about it. If people only had to eat between Thanksgiving and New Year's, everybody would have enough, because that's when we're all out there giving. If you can, help all year long and bring the same cheer home in July that you do in December.

Nonhumans need to eat, too, and the wise recognize the spiritual impact of feeding *all* those in need. My daughter and I experienced this in Nepal. We were staying in a modest hotel at the edge of Pokhara, in the Himalayan foothills. Beyond its fenced grounds were poverty and subsistence. It was on the side street just outside our lodgings that Rachael befriended a short-haired yellow dog: a skeletal apparition, she was clearly a female with puppies somewhere. Since we didn't eat the omelettes included with our hotel breakfast, Rachael started slipping them out to the dog in a self-styled doggy bag (a shower cap, as I recall).

The locals crowded around her every morning to witness the amazing ritual of offering food to a dog. Most of them were simply transfixed, as if they were watching some bizarre foreign stage show. A few seemed angry that she was feeding two valuable eggs to a mere dog when they themselves had nothing but rice and a few lentils for watery *dhal.*

The response of one woman, however, was distinctive. She looked as old as the mountains and the assembled group parted to allow her a clear view. She peered at Rachael with eyes so knowing that in them lack and riches seemed equally meaningless in light of something far greater than either of these. She placed her hands together as if to pray and nodded repeatedly to the child feeding the scrawny animal. *"Namaste,"* the old woman said over and over, a broad toothless smile showing her approval. *"Namaste, namaste, namaste."* Rachael wiped the grease on her tee-shirt, put her hands together in prayer position, bowed to the aged stranger, and replied, *"Namaste."*

*Namaste* is a word fraught with significance. Like *shalom* and *aloha,* it means "hello," "good-bye," and whatever else might be appropriate at the time. Its actual definition, however, is "I behold the divine in you." When you offer food to another being, the divine is apparent, in your home and in your heart.

Giving food is also wonderful practice for giving in other ways. There is so much history and culture around sharing food that doing it is a natural inclination for most of us. Yielding to that inclination helps us tap our innate generosity in all its aspects. Whatever and however you're comfortable giving, whether to a starving dog, a sick neighbor, or a homeless person you pass every day, the act of giving enriches not just you, and feeds not just that individual, but makes the world a better place for all of us.

Mystics of every time and tradition stress that there is a oneness to creation, that each of us is part of a greater whole. Albert Schweitzer put it this way: "Wherever you see life—that is you." The quantum physicists concur that as we share air and atoms and ozone, our lives are inextricably linked with all other lives. As neither a mystic nor a physicist, this is an incomprehensible concept to me—until I share something of myself, whether it's a dozen poems or a dozen cupcakes. In the giving, I catch a glimpse of that connectedness. And I remember why I feel such fondness for both my typewriter and my oven.

# 5
# Cleaning

When I was in sixth grade, my best friend, Rebecca Gott, and I decided to learn theology. During this flight of fancy, we read several books we didn't understand, including *The Practice of the Presence of God: The Complete Works of Brother Lawrence of the Resurrection*. Brother Lawrence was a seventeenth-century French mystic and monk assigned to work in the monastery kitchen. He would not "pick a straw up from the floor except for the love of God." He said, "I possess God in as great tranquility in the bustle of my kitchen—where sometimes several people are asking me for different things at once—as if I were on my knees at the Blessed Sacrament."

Usually, it must be admitted, Becky and I got more out of carrying around volumes of holy wisdom than actually reading them. (We liked feeling more sophisticated than our peers with their Nancy Drew mysteries.) Brother Lawrence's comments on domestic labor, however, did catch our attention. The implication was that we should carry out our household chores without complaint—that they were, in fact, to be dedicated to God. Perhaps not coincidentally, we didn't stay long with Brother Lawrence. We went on to Zen so we could contemplate the sound of one hand clapping—and continue to whine about chores with eleven-year-old abandon.

Sometimes I still whine about chores. Cleaning is boring, repetitive, mindless, unappreciated, physically demanding, sexually stereotyped, and societally undervalued. In this state of boredom, repetition, and mindlessness, however, we can be receptive to the divinity within us. Similarly, being called to an activity that is demanding, stereotyped, and undervalued can be used as an opportunity to gain humility. It can bring us face-to-face with the mystics' paradox: We are dust and we are divine. That's a lot to get from a sponge and a bucket.

Thich Nhat Hanh is a contemporary Buddhist monk, but like his seventeenth-century Christian counterpart Brother Lawrence, he is expert at finding the divine in the mundane. In his book *Peace Is Every Step,* he writes this of washing dishes: "I enjoy taking my time with each dish, being fully aware of the dish, the water, and each movement of my hands. I know that if I hurry in order to eat dessert sooner, the time of washing dishes will be unpleasant and not worth living. That would be a pity, for each minute, each second of life is a miracle. The dishes themselves and the fact that I am here washing them are miracles!"

Of course you and I aren't monks. We don't spend every day of our lives intently focused on realization of the divine. Precisely because we have so little time to concentrate on spiritual truth, it is all the more important for us to occasionally discover a little of that truth in a job we'd be doing anyway. In the everyday maintenance of our homes, we have the option of experiencing peace, contentment, and that safe feeling of being part of something large and grand and good.

"Action is eloquence," wrote Shakespeare, and the action we take in cleaning can be exquisitely eloquent when we let it. Having a clean house is secondary to the serenity that can be garnered from the physical act of cleaning itself. Cleanliness may be next to godliness, but an openness to the needs of living beings *is* godliness. While cleaning can be eloquent spiritual practice, obsessive concern over keeping a place clean is the opposite. Clean houses are fleeting—they last only until a biological being (other than the one with the dust cloth) enters the premises. I'm reminded of this every time I see those perfect pictures of interiors in magazines. Other than the occasional long-haired cat lounging on a miraculously unfurred sofa, those pictures don't have any living beings in them at all. This is understandable, of course, because living beings bring with them tracks, crumbs, spills, belongings, and more living beings (they're called friends) who in turn come equipped with their own dirt-compounding capabilities.

Since a clean house doesn't last, why even bother with one? I think it's because dust, clutter, and clothes asking to be laundered and ironed have something to teach us.

Eliminating dirt and disarray draws us into the rhythmic dance of sweeping and sorting, of washing a saucer or ironing a shirt, that is necessary and grounding. Most of us work with our brains all day and live in our heads the rest of the time. We read and think, compute and reason. Cleaning is physical, nonintellectual, and devoid of supertechnology. It deals with rudimentary elements like water and elbow grease. A friend told me that one night as she wiped out the tub after her bath, she had a revelation: "This is the most *real* thing I've done all day." I think that's often true for many of us.

Cleaning is definitely real and as old and as universal as praying. Some of my clearest travel memories involve seeing people cleaning: first in Lisbon when I was ten years old and saw women swabbing the airport floor with big string mops at 6 A.M. I felt sad for them because in my circumscribed world, women cleaned houses; men cleaned airports. But one of the women looked up from her work and gave me a welcoming smile I can still bring to mind. My world got bigger at that moment. When my own daughter was ten and we broke from our tour group to independently tramp through Shanghai, we met a charming grandmother proudly washing with a scrub brush the concrete floor of her tiny house. She put another border-erasing smile in my memory bank. And in Lhasa I stood mesmerized at a distance, watching a middle-aged monk doing laundry in a stream. His chore looked to me like a moving meditation.

Just as meditation can be healing for the body, cleaning can be healing for a house. It's taking away what doesn't belong to allow the beauty of what does belong to shine forth. This affects the lives of the people who live there: Even a relatively neat environment is conducive to both good living and clear thinking.

Relatively neat is, of course, relative. For some people, outward clutter reflects inner clutter; for others, perhaps, inner richness. If you live alone, you need only ascertain the level of cleanliness you want and what you will work (or pay someone else) to bring about. Living with other people is a bit more complicated; what is "lived in" to one person can look like *Tobacco Road* to somebody else. If you live with one or more people whose idea of cleanliness is less, let's say, developed than yours, make this compromise: Their private spaces—bedrooms, bathrooms, dens—are theirs. Your private spaces and any common spaces are yours. This means you'll be doing more cleaning than they will, but that's fair if you're the one who wants more cleanliness. Besides, you'll get all the benefits of cleaning as spiritual practice.

As much as I appreciate the process of cleaning, I am a clutterer by nature and I get a humility-packed reminder every so often. One of these I recall from my twenties when I worked for a local magazine. This was a society magazine, dealing with charity balls and debutantes. I knew it wasn't my life's work, but I wanted desperately to do a good job. At the end of every day, I made a list for the next one of leads to follow up on, stories that needed further editing, and appointments to confirm. One morning I came in to work (earlier than anybody else: I was dying to ace this job) and found that my boss had added an item to my list. It said, "Clean desk."

I was embarrassed and confused. Wasn't I the most dedicated editorial associate in the history of journalism? Didn't I do everything I was supposed to do and more besides? Wasn't my performance exemplary? Maybe. But I was still a slob. At that time, I thought everything was separate: I thought that subjecting my colleagues to my piles of papers and cups of decomposing tea bags didn't matter because I was a good worker.

I can't compartmentalize things so easily today. Everything seems too connected. My creativity and productivity are linked to the state of my surroundings, whether I want to believe that some days or not. Providing a pleasing environment for other people has less to do with their thinking ill of me if I don't (which they will), than with the fact that I owe those around me the respect of basic order. For me, basic order—a cleared chair to offer a guest, a clear pathway for walking, dishes washed from the last meal—is minimal. I actually prefer to have things somewhat neater than this, but expecting to keep them a great deal neater would mean taking attention from what I value more: things like family, friends, and writing this book.

Cleaning house is *not* the most important aspect of keeping house. It may not even make the top ten. Taking care of yourself, keeping your primary relationship close and communicative, being available to your children when they need you (not necessarily when it is convenient), and having an open door for everyone you care about are all more important than attacking dust bunnies, even those the size of Harvey. Once your priorities are set and living things take precedence over appearances, however, you can figure out where cleanliness fits in.

According to *feng shui*, even in a perfectly designed and furnished house, the life force cannot flow through a mess. The idea is that everything has its natural place. When that organic placement is respected, the human nervous system responds with a sense of calmness and peace. Looking around your house and seeing clean, harmonious spaces can make you feel that all's right with the world and your place in it. Your self-image looks as good to you then as your house does.

In fact, self-image and cleanliness are, for many people, closely linked. We take care of the things we care about. If our homes are essentially extensions of ourselves, then the energy we put into making them nurturing places says something about whether we feel we're worth that effort. Carol is a professional house cleaner who told me about the day it seemed so unfair that there were clean houses all over town because *she* cleaned them, but she didn't have the motivation to clean her own. "I said a prayer," she told me. "I said, 'God, help me to love and respect myself.' I kept repeating it like a mantra and I repeated it the whole time I cleaned my house. It gave me the energy to do the

work and in the end, I did feel that I loved and respected myself. I think part of that came from saying the prayer and part of it came from giving myself a clean house."

We can clean out of pride, compulsion, and concern about how other people see us, or we can do what Carol did and clean out of love and respect for ourselves, our families, even for the Creator of an orderly universe.

## Embracing the Broom

Because there comes a time in every life when the mop stops here, it would be a boon to civilization if more of us actually enjoyed mopping and similar chores. I think the reason we don't is not because housecleaning is inherently distasteful, but because we don't think that cleaning is part of our real lives. It's something to get through so we can get on to the things that count. But laundry and dishes *are* life. Shoveling the walk and mowing the lawn are life. Showing up for work in the morning and getting up with a sick child at night—add these up with a thousand activities like them and you get a life. Crucial to a satisfying one is to avoid rating each activity as if a lifetime were some extended Sweeps Week.

If cleaning is a problem, solve the problem. Since its certainty is right up there with death and taxes, find ways to make it enjoyable. The following suggestions are designed to help if you feel short on time, skill, or enthusiasm for cleaning. These should also help you brainstorm additional solutions of your own.

LACK OF TIME: Get some help (see the upcoming section, "Help at Hand") or rethink your priorities. Do you have to keep your house as clean as you now believe you do? Does thinking it has to be perfect freeze you in your tracks and either keep you from cleaning at all or make you dissatisfied with the results? Would a change of decor make cleaning easier? (Taking up the white carpeting may seem like major surgery, but if you have three preschoolers and a black Lab, the surgery could be lifesaving.) Have you sufficiently simplified to reduce the demands on your time? You can even ask yourself the seemingly radical question, "Do members of this household really need to work as many hours as we do?" The sky won't fall just because you ask the question.

There are also ways to keep a cleaner home that take no time. If you can encourage people to take off their shoes when they come in, you can cut your cleaning time by a third. Most dirt and dust in a house get there off people's shoes. One couple I know had a woodworker make them a lovely rack for the specific purpose of housing the shoes of anyone entering. They don't need to mention it; the rack says it all.

Another way to cut cleaning time is by playing Fifty-two Pick-Up a couple of times a day. Choose any number (fifty-two is pushing it—fifteen or twenty is more realistic) and pick up that number of items around your house. You can count a dish put away, a newspaper folded, a coat hung up, or a book returned to the shelf. This is also a good game for getting kids involved, although they're likely to say, "I picked up seventeen things and five of them were yours."

Fifty-two Pick-Up or your favored method of regularly getting the better of gravity is essential because picking up isn't as soul-satisfying as actual cleaning, and it can take a lot more time. Professional cleaners can do a good-size house in three hours, when it might take the owner of the house three days. Why? When it's your house, you pick things up as you go. You put them away.

You dust them off. And if you're like me, you dawdle. When the picking up is done daily, though, cleaning is a breeze.

**LACK OF SKILL:** Some people simply don't know how to clean. I didn't. We had a housekeeper when I was growing up and other than a few basic jobs I had to do to earn my allowance, I never learned how to clean efficiently. It took me hours to get through one room, leaving me too discouraged to go on to the next.

When I was young, I dated a fellow whose way to win my heart was to come over and help clean my apartment. It worked. I figured he and I would go off into the sunset with stars in our eyes and a Hoover in his hand. We didn't. But I still had the vacuum and its operating manual. I also knew a woman with a housecleaning business who taught me how to clean for myself. She said I only had to be willing to do the job quickly, imperfectly, and without emotional investment.

"You have to pretend you're cleaning someone else's house," she said. "Stack anything that hasn't been picked up. Don't read the magazine, answer the letter, or play with the Frisbee. Just stack the stuff and clean. Do the bathroom first since nobody likes that job. Do the kitchen next while you still have energy. Dust before you vacuum and then go home." I reminded her that I was already there.

**LACK OF ENTHUSIASM:** Cleaning can be drudgery, but it doesn't have to be. I can remember times—very few, but I remember them—of being so jubilant about something or other that I cleaned like a house afire. What I have to do on ordinary cleaning days when I am substantially less motivated is supply myself with some of that energy.

Sometimes I do it by wearing brightly colored clothes. (A research project showed that exercisers had more stamina when they wore red leotards.) Or I put on an apron because my childhood imprinting was that people clean in aprons. It's a uniform my psyche can relate to. And I often play energetic music. A German saying goes, "Music wipes away the dust of everyday living," and I can use all the help dusting I can get. There is a particular rock tape I use for this so consistently that once when the band was on TV, my daughter called them "that cleaning group."

Using the right materials to clean with can put me in a more willing mood as well. If you're athletic, you know how quality sports equipment can make a difference in your game. It's even more important to have good cleaning equipment, because you like golf or tennis but you probably don't like to clean.

Take brooms, for instance. In old Europe, they were considered sacred, and in Chinese folklore there is even a broom goddess named Sao Ch'ing Niang. I have a broom that was handmade in the Ozarks of colored straw, carefully tied together. Sacred may be too strong an adjective, but it's an awfully nice broom. I like how it looks, how it feels, and how it sweeps.

I am also partial to cleaning with serious equipment from a janitorial supply house or well-equipped hardware store. There you can find dust pans wide enough to be genuinely helpful, real squeegees instead of toys, and substantial string mops that can handle most kitchens with one dunk in the water bucket. (My bucket is a double one, by the way: one side for the cleaning solution, one side for rinsing.)

I realize that sponges, dust mops, scrub brushes, and their kin are not commonly on display in art museums, but for me to have enough enthusiasm to enjoy cleaning my house, the ones I use have to be aesthetically agreeable to me. I don't mind wiping the kitchen counters, for instance, when I use one of those French pop-up sponges. They are flat wafers when you buy them but expand and soften with their first introduction to water. And they're not dyed to be any color other than their own creamy beige.

Of course, I think even the lowly cleaning rag can be beautiful. Saving scraps of fabric for this purpose has been resurrected by the environmental movement as preferable to paper towels and toss-away wipes. A soft cotton rag feels good in your hand. It lets a long-loved shirt reincarnate. And it reminds me of my grandmother and her rag bag.

## Help at Hand

Since realizing that cleaning can be both a sensuous and spiritual exercise, I've actually come to enjoy it. It might surprise you that I have a cleaning person anyway. Getting this kind of help is not self-indulgence. It is time management. I spend about two hours a day on cooking, dishes, laundry, ironing, and general household maintenance. Carol comes on alternate Thursdays to do the rest. I look at having her clean my house the way I look at having the dentist clean my teeth: I do the daily stuff; she does the deep cleaning. I didn't hire Carol because I don't know how to clean or because I detest it. I hired her because at this time in my life, I have other priorities.

There was a time when I might not have told you that because I would have thought it sounded too la-di-da. I suppose I felt like the boss I used to have who explained to her staff that she left the office early twice a week to see her therapist. We thought she had some serious emotional problem to require such intensive therapy on a long-term basis. Then we learned that this therapist was a *massage* therapist. We all asked for raises.

But just as many people now realize the benefits of massage, lots of us have also found that the increased quality of life a cleaning person can provide easily justifies the expense, even when another luxury is given up to pay for it. Working women led the way on this, which makes sense, but there's no reason a stay-at-home wife—or husband—can't have cleaning help, too. If you can be of greater value to your family by spending more time with your children and truly *making* a home rather than just cleaning one, look into fitting a house cleaner into your budget. There are a variety of ways to find a good person. Check the rates of cleaning services in the Yellow Pages. Their prices are usually higher than those of independent cleaners, but not necessarily. Services are generally reliable, guarantee their work, and have bonded employees.

I like independent cleaners myself. I identify with their entrepreneurial spirit. The best way to locate a gem is to ask friends for recommendations. Ask everyone. If they've never said they have cleaning help, they may be keeping it to themselves like my boss and her massages. If you can't find someone this way, run an ad in a weekly shopper or put up a flyer at a neighborhood church, market, or community center. Interview the person first and get references, especially if she (or he) will come while you're away and need a key to your place.

Be sure you understand each other. Carol let me know up front that she would not clean the oven or the inside of the refrigerator unless I asked her on the days I wanted it done. She told me she cleaned surfaces and wouldn't move furniture. I told her I wanted her to use my environmentally friendly cleaning products. We had a deal.

Most cleaning people who are independent contractors rather than your personal employees will not pick up and put away, arrange your drawers, or organize your desk. Many will not wash dishes or make beds. Forget basements and attics, although a dedicated cleaning person like Carol might spruce up the screened porch and surprise you. Similarly, walls, windows, and intensive spring cleaning are up to you, a service specializing in heavy-duty jobs, or by special arrangement with your cleaner.

A cleaning person's expertise is those areas of the house that are readily visible. When you walk through, you experience the beauty of every room's being clean at the same time. The floors are mopped, the carpets are vacuumed, and the kitchen counters, sinks, and appliance exteriors sparkle. The bathroom is pristine, the bedrooms neat, and if she or he uses the right cleaning products, your house smells great, too.

If this sounds heavenly but extravagant, consider a low- or no-cost cleaner. Some high school and college students would rather clean houses than flip burgers and will do so for a reasonable fee. You can also trade cleaning with a friend: you do her house, she does yours. When you clean a place you're not emotionally involved with, the temptation to get caught up in details is removed. That can save more time than the trip to her house takes. You might be able to barter other services, too: you could baby-sit or teach your friend Spanish or tutor her son in algebra in return for cleaning.

## Polishing a Planet

Whether you're cleaning or someone else is, the sweeping and scrubbing don't take place in a void. Your house or apartment is part of a community and an ecosystem. It's not inert; it's vital and interactive. It affects everyone who lives there and they affect it. This home exists out of the hospitality of Mother Earth. One way to respect her, the house, and its inhabitants is by using cleaning products that are natural, nontoxic, and biodegradable.

There are known toxins in the majority of commercial cleansers. These are believed to be safe when properly used, but the long-term results of contact with them has not been definitively studied. If cleaning products were the only questionable chemicals we ever associated with, this might be a moot point. But exposure to pesticides, industrial and automotive pollution, chlorinated water, and food additives is also part of contemporary life.

Cleaning your house with nontoxic products will give you better indoor air and does not contribute to the burden of pollutants everybody breathes. Besides, like pop-up sponges and cotton rags, natural cleansers are really pleasurable to work with. You can buy such products ready-made at a natural foods store, or concoct your own easily and inexpensively. In the same way that baking bread or making curtains has a lovely feeling of domesticity, so does making simple cleaning supplies. They just take less time and no talent.

Ingredients for simple cleaning supplies are obtainable at any grocery store—things like baking soda, washing soda, vinegar, borax, lemon juice, salt, cornstarch, and club soda. It can actually be fun to play chemist with all this stuff. The "lab manual" I recommend is Annie Berthold-Bond's readable and informative book *Clean & Green*. It covers not only standard cleaning aids but air fresheners, jewelry cleaners, laundry preparations, and cleansers for everything from hairbrushes to automobiles to piano keys. All the formulations are simple and call for virtually no esoteric ingredients.

I keep my homemade cleansers exceedingly elementary. On

windows, for instance, I use distilled vinegar and water in a spray bottle. (Berthold-Bond suggests one eighth cup vinegar to one cup water.) Vinegar and water (a cup to a pail, according to the expert) cleans tile and linoleum. If I'm out of Bon Ami, an environmentally innocent scouring powder, I use plain old baking soda. It can clean toilet bowls, stainless steel sinks, refrigerators, and—with boiling water—drains. I've used it to deal with pet odors on rugs, and little bowls of it absorb unpleasant smells in the fridge, freezer, and closets. (If you ever wondered who buys those industrial-size boxes of baking soda, I do.)

A legitimate question would certainly be, "Does this stuff work or does your house look as if it's been doused in salad dressing and muffin dough?" It does work. Cleaning is a chemical (product) and mechanical (elbow grease) operation. The chemical does not have to be harsh or synthetic to do the job.

Working with kitchen solutions and gentle commercial products cleans on another level as well: It keeps your home's connection to nature strong and pure. You know how you resonate to real marble and natural wood in a way you just don't to some reasonable facsimile? People resonate in a similar way to a house cleaned with natural products that are compatible with healthy living and a healthy planet. When you walk in and notice how clean your house smells, it won't be because it reminds you of the pool at the Y. It will be more like a morning in the mountains.

## How to Clean Like Brother Lawrence

With natural cleansers and cotton cloths, a little music and a lighthearted view of the assignment, cleaning your house can be a joy. With the right frame of mind, it can take you all the way to blissful. Bliss isn't exactly synonymous with happiness. We're usually happy because of some outside event: "He called!" "We won!" "I'm invited!" Bliss is more an understated, nonstop happiness for no reason at all. People experience this when they are in touch with the divine essence that runs throughout all creation. In simple chores around the house, the body is occupied so the mind is free to drift toward bliss.

This is how Brother Lawrence became so content in his menial tasks: He learned to see God in each one. For him, each act of everyday life was a means of "practicing the presence of God." We practice this presence—which is always with us and which can go by any name we wish to give it—by temporarily letting go of the personal ego to embrace something all-encompassing. We can do this in many ways. Among them are meditation, creativity, and cleaning the basement. I have a suspicion that Brother Lawrence cleaned rather like children do. (I don't think that's an insult to Brother Lawrence: Jesus himself said that becoming like a child is indispensable for entering the kingdom of heaven.)

When children in Montessori preschools are allowed to choose the area in which they'll work, the most popular is invariably "practical life"—comprised largely of cleaning activities. The children relish the process and see only good results. The streaks and missed places are invisible to them. They enjoy the activity and they pronounce the results good. We, too, can enjoy cleaning and pronounce the results good enough.

You can do an experiment to see how this works. Try it first with some household chore that you like—or at least one that you don't despise. For some people, this is washing dishes, for others sweeping or mopping, dusting furniture or polishing silver. For me, it's ironing. Ironing is calming to me, and I love seeing a wrinkly mass become a wearable garment.

Whatever task you choose, decide that during this particular time of doing it, you are going to focus on the process of transformation that you're engaged in. I realize it's a stretch. We don't often think of scouring a pot as transformative, but it is. It's a kind of restoration. Admittedly, this isn't restoring the Sistine Chapel ceiling, but it is restoring a pot back to the way its designer envisioned it, back to beauty and usefulness.

For the sake of experiment, allow yourself to scrub this pot or polish this table as pure experience. Be with the cloth. Be with the object being cleaned. Allow yourself to experience feelings of lightheartedness, freedom, gratitude, and unity. You may have these feelings and you may not. Just don't keep them away intentionally by telling yourself, "This is cleaning and cleaning stinks."

Be sure to give yourself a time limit—thirty minutes is good. Then reflect on what you did and how it felt. If you keep a journal, write about this exercise. If you liked the experience, or if it felt even a little better than cleaning usually does, do it again. Do it for up to thirty minutes of the time you spend cleaning. Eventually, you'll find that this is more and more the way you do your housework. The presence of God is here because the presence of God is everywhere. As Tennyson wrote, "Closer is He than breathing, and nearer than hands and feet." This presence is in simple activities that quiet us down and help us remember.

In addition, of course, we get to look around at the place we've spiffed and polished and see it at its best. It was like that for me one Saturday when David, a colleague of mine, dropped by to critique a speech I was working on. He had never been to my house before, so I did the usual straightening up that first-time visitors inspire. I dusted and vacuumed, after first removing from my living room a wicker laundry basket's worth of miscellany—the scissors that belong upstairs, the hats and gloves that belong in a closet, and my daughter's 130 Chinese character flash cards that belong somewhere besides on a windowsill. When David walked in, he said, "What a *beautiful* house!" I know he meant it because of the way he emphasized "beautiful." It was easy to say "thank you," because when my house is clean, I think it's beautiful, too.

Shortly after my meeting with David, two of Rachael's friends came to call. They brought their dog to play with our dog. The girls made guacamole. Then they made snack bars out of oats and dates and shredded coconut and maple syrup. After that they played board games, the ones with little pieces that magnetically affix to everything except the box they came in. Before long, the house looked like it usually does, a place where people live. And I thought as I sat in the midst of it, with a steaming cup of tea and a really luscious snack bar, that keeping a home in order is like keeping a life in order. The process is continual. It doesn't end. I can resent that or relish it.

# 6
# Celebrating

A friend of mine has a glorious old house with a ballroom on the third floor. It even has an intercom, circa 1911: a tube running through the wall from the ballroom to the main kitchen, so the servants could be apprised of what delicacies were running low upstairs. It's been some time since that house saw servants and formal dances, but my daughter borrowed the third-floor space for her twelfth birthday party. It would be a pity to let a perfectly good ballroom go to waste.

While the original owner of this house was able to include such a room because of his privilege, I love the idea of a house built with ample space designated for celebration. Celebration is a spiritual necessity, and feasts and joyous rituals are at least as old as recorded history. These don't require servants and ballrooms, of course, only people. This is because souls thrive on community. Solitude can hasten spiritual growth, but isolation can impede it.

Our homes need revelry as much as we do. Few things enliven a residence as thoroughly as giving it a reputation for celebration. Every holiday marked there, every congratulatory dinner, every open house honoring visitors from away—these add up to make your house or apartment a place that radiates warmth, hospitality, and memories by the roomful.

When we're bogged down by the complications of life, work, family, finances, home maintenance, health maintenance, community commitments, and the rest, celebrating can sound like an invitation to more work. But celebrations come in all sizes. Modest expectations are a godsend. They allow an ordinary dinner, accompanied by stemmed goblets or a rose in a vase, to become a celebration.

There are quiet, spiritual celebrations as well: lighting Shabbat candles or saying the rosary every evening in the living room. If you grew up with such an observance, you might consider resurrecting it today, perhaps in an amended or abbreviated form. Many people say, "I'm not religious, I'm spiritual," but take a close look at that word: spi/ritual. Incorporating into your life a ritual you might cherish does not require that you buy a theology wholesale or align yourself with a religious institution in any way that is uncomfortable for you. It simply means enjoying the beauty of your heritage. When this kind of ritual feels natural and becomes something you look forward to, your home itself will take hold of that spirit and become a more soothing, refreshing place.

## The Art of the Gathering

I prefer the word *gathering* to *party*. Parties imply paper hats and noisemakers, and when "party" is used as a verb, it's a synonym for "drink too much." A gathering, on the other hand, puts the emphasis where it belongs—on the people who are gathered to enjoy one another's company. Having a gathering, or a party if you like, doesn't take the perfect house, wardrobe, cuisine, or hall-decking capabilities. And you don't have to have great bunches of congenial friends; as long as you avoid sworn enemies, people will find something to talk about and be responsible for their own good time.

Practically speaking, a successful gathering needs a theme or focus, something to eat and drink, and logistical trouble-shooting done in advance. The theme is simply the raison d'être for the get-together. If it's a bridal shower, people know to bring a gift. If it's a pool party, they'll know to bring swimwear. When you keep the focus in mind, you can keep the planning simple and arrive at your own gathering relaxed enough to enjoy it.

The food can be a full meal, munchies, or dessert. You don't have to cook all day; there is help available from the deli counter, caterers, or the pragmatic marvel of the potluck. You have this kind of choice regarding beverages, too: full bar, beer and wine, or teetotaler toasts. My personal choice is not to serve alcohol at my gatherings, and it's never caused anyone to refuse an invitation.

As for logistics, ease your mind by deciding in advance where coats will be put, where the pets will be, what rooms will be open to guests, and whether you'll do all the preparation and cleanup yourself or get help. (Students looking for extra cash are often eager to help with serving and the like. Cohosting with a friend can also cut the workload.)

In addition to formal gatherings with this kind of advance planning, there are those that come together on their own. One Sunday we were having a young fashion designer we know over for lunch and to look at some of Rachael's sketches. That morning a call came in from one of Rachael's friends who needed help with a school project. The guest list for lunch grew to include this girl and her parents as well. We never set out to have a "party"—there wasn't a paper hat in sight—but we ended up with a marvelous gathering just the same.

Gatherings with some work to do—in this case, a lesson in pattern-making and proofreading a paper for English—can be the best. I think most of us have a certain fascination with pioneers' quilting bees and the barn raisings the Amish have to this day. Gatherings with a purpose have an appeal ordinary parties seldom match. A house blessing, like the one described in chapter two, has a purpose. So do valentine-making, pizza-baking, tree-trimming, and taffy-pulling affairs.

Gatherings to meet an exceptional person or hear an intriguing idea are wonderful, too. We once had as house guests both a doctor of Tibetan medicine and a natural healer from Denmark who had just left her post in the royal court of Oman. The gathering to meet with them was a combination world tour and exercise in paradigm-shifting. It's tough to stay stuck in a restricted outlook in the presence of someone from a vastly different culture. This continual revision of our perspective takes place whenever we interact with other people. The world as seen by someone from another neighborhood can sometimes be almost as different as that perceived by someone from another hemisphere.

An ideal gathering, then—from the vantage point of a home and a soul—is one that includes people of different ages, races, religions, professions, and lifestyles. This doesn't mean checking a guest list to be sure it has a "token grandfather" or a "token attorney." It's realizing that any guest list is an abridged roster of the people in your life. Do you segregate yourself with those who are just like you, or do you give yourself, your family, and your home the privilege of genuinely mixed company?

The near quarantine of the elderly is perhaps the most

poignant illustration of our society's inability to accept all its members. In earlier times, and right now in other places, grandparents and great-grandparents were part of every family event. Their wisdom was revered and their skills were valued. Rachael's only living grandparent lives far away from us. We see her when we can. At other times, we have friends of advanced years to share in our gatherings. Friends with toddlers who make a mess and cause our cats to glare at us in disdain come, too, along with other people who bring their own intangible gifts and their stories.

Literal stories and the telling of them can have an important place at gatherings as well. People's lives are filled with inspiring and instructive tales, and all religions and cultures have great stories with universal applications. One day we were having lunch at the home of friends when Jagat, a father of three and an inimitable storyteller, shared a yarn from the Mahabarata, an ancient Indian epic. It seems that in the battle between the forces of good and evil, the evil warriors very nearly won. A young soldier from the side of light asked his superior how, even without good on his side, their opponent had been so powerful. The superior told him to ask the question directly of the erstwhile enemy, but to ask it with respect. So the youthful fighter approached the dying leader of the opposition forces and asked how it was that, even without good on his side, he had almost won the battle. "My power comes," the fallen warrior told him, "because everything I have to do I do today. And everything I have to do today, I do now."

Although there were children present—four of them, aged three to thirteen—no one had asked for a story. Its telling grew naturally from the situation and those of us seated around the table. At our various stages of life and into our separate circumstances, we took that story and made it ours. I've heard the children speak of it since, and I've applied it to my own life when I've wanted to put something off.

So gather some people around you and let your experiences blend with theirs. They may bring flowers or a candle or a bottle of wine, but those gifts aren't the ones that will live on in your house as long as you do. The gift of each individual's presence is that lasting, though. Adding the good cheer of friends to objects that inspire you, simplified space, delicious food, and lovingly maintained surroundings will result in the sort of place your soul will want to come home to.

## Celebrating Ordinary Days

For celebration to become your instinctive response to life and the hallmark of your home takes a well-honed sense of wonder. People who celebrate spontaneously and without affectation do it because they know there is always something to celebrate. And they're right: The holiest of holidays is really this one, this day, because it's the one we've got to work with. To say that we should celebrate just being alive sounds as corny as a bowl of polenta, but like so much maize-tinted wisdom, it is absolutely true.

Every religion and philosophy has its own explanation of human life, but all agree on its sanctity and its value. There is a Buddhist story that asks us to imagine a wooden ring—an embroidery hoop, let's say—tossed into a vast ocean. We are then to imagine a blind sea turtle that comes to the surface of the ocean only once every one hundred years. That blind turtle, the lesson says, is as likely to surface through the embroidery hoop as we are to have a chance at life on earth. This life is rare and precious. Celebrating that we have a day of it to live is neither mindless nor simplistic.

To celebrate a day that appears to have nothing worth celebrating, you can honor its course by staying within it. Keep your attention on this day, its charms and obligations, and forget about the yesterdays and tomorrows. When you focus on the present moment, you start to see as Walt Whitman did that "every hour of the light and dark is a miracle, every cubic inch of space is a miracle." Seeing this is celebrating at the most profound and personal level. When you get the hang of it, it's as if you always have some wonderful secret. You become one of those people who is generally happy, one of those people you may have resented, or at least misunderstood, before.

You can bring this celebration of ordinary days into your home with a fresh flower or a bouquet, candles lit or a fire laid, moving around the furniture, or bringing out a print or painting that has been stored and retiring one that has been on display. (The Chinese have recommended this practice since ancient times to keep the eye from tiring of a work of art.) Decorate an average day with festive food—a pie or a watermelon. Dance with your spouse, your child, or your stereo. If your newspaper lists birthdays of the famed and notorious, it's somebody's today. Have an appropriately themed minifête.

One of our best celebrations was an impromptu birthday party for Mozart. Rachael was eight and quite taken with the thought of someone her age composing, so on the draggy winter afternoon— January 27, to be exact—that the newspaper told us was his birthday, we played Mozart tapes and baked a sheet cake. There was some half-used cake decorating gel left over from the birthday of someone still living, so we used it to regale Wolfgang's cake in quarter notes and sharps and flats. Then we rented the film *Amadeus*. A week later I overheard Rachael asking one of her friends what he had done for Mozart's birthday. Holidays are in the home of the beholder. We now do Mozart's birthday every year.

The four seasons provide ample fodder for deviation from routine, along with affording us the comfort of seasonal routines themselves. You might celebrate the first daffodil in your spring garden by buying a bunch of them from the florist. You could celebrate summer's first strawberries with a trip to the farmer's market, making shortcake, or simply serving berries from the basket, dipped if you like in confectioner's sugar. Celebrate the return to school in the fall by making a big deal out of shopping for school supplies, or restocking pens and pencils and paper for your own desk.

Welcome the first snowfall by making paper snowflakes with your kids and snow ice cream for any takers. They said when I was a child that snow had become radioactive, but I don't glow in the dark yet, in spite of a yearly treat of the first snow mixed with maple sugar, vanilla, and cream (actually, I use soy milk now and the fun is in no way diminished). Eating snow ice cream in my big chair by the west window is absolutely splendid. I watch the weather do its show and if there are kids around, one invariably says, "Maybe we'll get snowed in." Even though I know that where we live snow often melts the next day, I say, "Maybe we will," and really hope it happens.

If your locale is one without distinct seasonal weather changes, be aware of the subtle ones that mark the order of the year. As human beings, we have a long history of basing our lives on nature's patterns. Even if you spend most of your days in an office building with windows that don't open, be sure that on your days and nights at home you notice a budding crocus, a turning leaf, a crescent moon. The soul yearns for recognition of nature. This is true even for those of us who aren't "nature people." It's not just the folks with hiking boots and camping gear who are affected by nature's cycles and subject to nature's laws.

Let your home be seasonal, with its colors and sights and scents revolving as the earth does through her primeval passages. Acknowledge spring by bringing in some pussy willow and changing dark linens and wall hangings for pastels. Salute summer with whites and open windows, autumn with russet tones and cider simmering, winter with chairs turned toward the fireplace, the smell of pine, and the coziness of afghans and long novels.

## Sabbath

When I was growing up, most retailers were closed on Sundays and stores that were open had much of their merchandise covered in compliance with the "blue laws." I found the whole thing a colossal nuisance. It seemed absurd that a day was set aside to keep people from buying things. Now that we can buy anything we like on Sunday, though, there is an increasing trend toward refraining from doing so. I meet more and more people as I travel who keep Sunday—or Saturday or Friday depending upon religious background and personal inclination—a day apart.

The first person to let me in on this was a speaker at a conference who said he was honored to be in the program, but he regretted that the meeting was taking place on Saturday. He explained that keeping Saturday for reverence and reflection was part of his Jewish faith, and that he had also expanded the idea of Sabbath to include reverence for the earth and all life on it. On Saturdays, he was committed to polluting less by not driving his car. He ate lightly and simply of locally grown foods. He didn't work but he did play, and he contemplated divine ideas and their effect on his life.

As he spoke, the room was so quiet you could have heard someone else's conscience. In a diverse and largely secular audience, he had struck a chord. Each of us knew we needed a genuine day off and couldn't remember when we'd last taken one. Although I can't even recall now what his actual talk was about, the caveat with which he introduced it changed the way I look at life—and what I do with weekends.

All I could do at first to make Sunday restful was refrain from turning on my word processor. That way at least I wasn't working for money, even if I did sneak in a load of laundry. This evolved over time into a genuine day of rest, a day that has enriched my relationships, increased my creativity, and substantially improved my health. I think I used to get colds because I wouldn't get off the overachievement treadmill any other way. I don't catch cold as readily anymore. And I love Sunday now; it's the one day I don't have to produce. I can just experience.

I don't spend all day Sunday at home—we go to church and often out to eat or to a movie or play or concert—but what I do with Sunday's home hours is most telling. Can I be at home without being hell-bent on making check marks on a to-do list? It is a challenge. To help out, I have a another list, one of Sunday pastimes, to refer to: board games, potluck dinners, picnics, a long yoga set, reading for pleasure or inspiration, taking advantage of low long-distance rates, practicing calligraphy, brushing the cats, playing with the dog, giving myself a facial, and seeing people who make me happy.

Sabbath is a gift you give yourself. If you have a Jewish or Christian background, remember that even God rested: you can, too. If you have no religious reason for honoring a Sabbath, take one of your days off and make it personally sacrosanct, a day to do what you want to instead of what you have to. I know this is difficult to do if you work long hours and you have only two days in the week for marketing and laundry and errands and housework. But devoting a day to your faith and yourself and your family is a magical expenditure that, like tithing your time, will return to you in inexplicable ways.

Did you make the list back in chapter three of all the things you want to do before you die? That list probably didn't have on it, "Get the car tuned up" and "Stop at the post office." You'll do those things, but on the day you set aside to celebrate life itself, do something else. Look at the list you made. When will you get around to rock climbing and writing your memoirs? If you set aside a day each week for your soul to play, you'll get around to them this weekend.

There's another bonus in observing a bona fide day off: You'll be noticeably more prolific when you're working. For this boon to take place, you need to learn to not even *think* about work on the day you've set aside. Once you get this down, you'll find that you go back to the office truly refreshed. Mondays will start looking better. And you'll resent your work less every day of the week because you'll know there's one day when it simply does not exist.

## Special Days

Observing a Sabbath punctuates the week, compelling us to pause for a bit. It keeps the days from blurring together and makes us more mindful of the passage of time. Holidays serve the same purpose, only more boldly. If Sabbath is a dash, holidays are exclamation points—they get our attention. While they don't cause our busyness to cease, they channel it in a different and, hopefully, joyful direction.

Holidays prompt us to focus on home, if only to hang a sprig of mistletoe in December or hoist the Stars and Stripes in early July. During a regular week, home can seem like little more than the starting line for a relay race: Bang! And they're off—to work, classes, meetings, the orthodontist's, the fix-it shop, the gym, the drugstore, the grocer's, the mall. Around holidays, we may be doing all this and more, but our focus shifts: Home no longer serves the going out; the going out serves home.

We do see home and holidays differently at different times in our lives. Young people tend to go back to Mom's for holidays, and the thought of doing a major feast in their own digs is often too daunting to consider. This isn't an absolute, of course: I made Thanksgiving dinner in my studio apartment when I was nineteen and single. I wasn't a vegetarian yet, but I didn't trust myself to cook a turkey. Instead I baked eight Rock Cornish game hens and felt that this accomplishment aged me decades. *That* kind of cooking was what somebody's mother did.

It is true that having children—and to an extent just getting married—make holidays at home an important event. The big dinner may be at the folks' or the in-laws', but fashioning traditions at home for part of the day or part of the season suddenly becomes crucial in a way it may never have been before. Whether in response to the mandate of parenthood or simply as an experiment at any stage of life, celebrating holidays at home creates special memories. As a result, we come to cherish in a special way the place where those memories developed.

At our house, we celebrate Christmas from Saint Nicholas Day to Epiphany, and we "start over" at the Jewish New Year, Chinese New Year, and the conventional New Year. Although we are neither Jewish, Chinese, nor conventional, a month without a holiday is a long month.

We also devise a bit of merriment for Kwanzaa, Mardi gras, and every equinox and solstice. Our annual valentine-making party is a multigenerational mélange of lace and doilies and red crepe paper, and we always read the story of the miracle of Saint Valentine, who, while imprisoned by the Romans, is said to have restored the sight of his jailer's blind daughter. Every year on Rachael's birthday, I make her favorite food: Ethiopian. It takes me all day and uses more cooking oil than I generally go through in three weeks. It's great. It's our tradition.

I come by my holiday spirit honestly: Both my mother and father were intent on marking occasions. There were home movies for the first day of school, elaborate picnics on the Fourth of July, and major productions for birthdays and Christmas. The intensity of these celebrations did not diminish after my parents' divorce, much to their credit and my benefit.

Some of the people I admire most, however, make short shrift of birthdays and holidays. They decry the materialism, the shoddy decorations, the environmentally costly excesses, and loss of true meaning in the rush to give gifts instead of time. I understand their frustration, but regardless of what society does with a day, any one of us can do with it what we like. Holidays do not have to be times for doing what everybody else does or what you've always done before. They can be a springboard for creative celebration.

If you're a single person on your own, you can create appropriate festivities from scratch. If you're part of a couple or if you have children, you can formulate traditions that just might last a lifetime. Believe me, if anyone had predicted ten years ago that customs would grow up around me involving Ethiopian cuisine and cakes for dead composers, I would have told them to take their crystal ball to the repair shop. But made-to-order traditions naturally take shape in a home once you're open to them.

I know it's not always easy or even possible to have precisely the kind of holiday you would design. Because we're connected to other people, holidays can ask that we observe rituals—religious or commercial—that are not in alignment with our worldview. They can also cause us to spend time with family members who push every emotional panic button we've got. On the other hand, if we're estranged from our families or unable for one reason or another to be with them on what are supposed to be "family days," we lament the separation. With such a definitive no-win situation, it's little wonder some people would rather forget holidays altogether. That is one option. But there is benefit for our homes and our souls in taking a different tack.

The key to appreciating any holiday is to accept it as it is. The fireworks might be duds or the crust on the pumpkin pie could burn, and there's no telling what some relative might say or do, but as long as the day isn't too heavily orchestrated, you can enjoy it anyway. Tradition is worth preserving, but we frustrate ourselves when we expect things to always be the same. Comparing one year's holiday to another's is asking for trouble, because we tend to view the past through rose-colored glasses. If we don't compare our celebrations to another year's or another person's, every holiday can be memorable in its uniqueness.

I learned this from a Christmas several years ago and it applies to all holidays. This was the first Christmas of our Ozarks exodus. I decided we'd have a better time with friends in the city than by ourselves in the country so we drove two hundred miles to become the Christmas Eve house guests of a family we knew back in Kansas City. My little girl awakened early the next morning and was eager to get started on Christmas. Not wanting to disturb our

hosts who were sleeping in, I told Rachael we'd go out for breakfast. Every one of the dozen morning spots I knew of was closed for
the holiday, so we were reduced to aimless driving—not exactly
inspiring under any circumstances, and on Christmas Day thoroughly depressing.

Finally, just across the state line between Missouri and Kansas,
we found an open truckers' café. "This is the pits," I thought to
myself. "While other kids are thinking of a flying sleigh, you are
stuck with eighteen-wheelers." I reluctantly held the door open for
Rachael, expecting to join a few lost souls drinking coffee and looking as sad as I felt. But going through that door was like going
through the looking glass with Alice: We entered a parallel universe where people could be happy spending Christmas in a truck
stop. This place was packed, and everybody in it was *celebrating*.

The jukeboxes cranked out Christmas carols and the fry cooks
cranked out hotcakes. People were wishing us Merry Christmas
and giving Rachael candy canes. I thought we'd intruded on a private party. "No, hon," a woman said when I asked. "This is everybody's party." She explained that since trucking doesn't halt for
Christmas, drivers' families meet them on the road. Those without
family nearby become part of somebody else's for a while. Nobody
seemed to mind taking on this Toyota driver and her child, too.

To appreciate that most unusual Yuletide, I had to let go of my
insistence that a good Christmas *had* to be with lots of family and
a brandied fruitcake. That's one kind of good Christmas; this was
another. When we arrived at our friends' house after breakfast,
they were getting up. We lingered over Christmas presents—three
kids under eight can stretch out those proceedings considerably—
and I helped with Christmas dinner. The day with our friends was
lovely, and the morning with the truckers was priceless.

Since then I've had a lot of picture-perfect holidays at home and I cherish each one. I have also, however, had a few that would never be mistaken for a Currier and Ives print. We spent one Thanksgiving in India with Rachael confined to bed with bronchitis. We ate lentil burgers from room service, but since the management knew we were Americans they put little turkey-and-pilgrim place cards on the tray. Then there was the Halloween in China, which we recognized with a stop at a candy store and the discovery of a caramel-like confection called White Rabbit. Now we buy White Rabbit at a Chinese market for our own trick-or-treaters.

When the festivities of a holiday take place at your house, you're like the director of a film or a play; you have a fair amount of control. When you're somewhere else, you're more like an actor in someone else's production. That's why it's good that holidays happen every year: Sometimes you'll host them and other times you won't. Go graciously from one to the other.

Regardless of the outward way you'll spend some holiday or other, keep it in your heart exactly as you want it. If this is a day of spiritual significance to you, feast heartily on spiritual food. If it's a day for reflection and preparation, like your birthday or New Year's Day, find some time for yourself and a place to be quiet in the midst of the hubbub. If your soul longs for a certain observance that isn't taking place, see that it does—even if you make it a postscripted celebration the next day or the next week.

Find out, if you can, what other souls are seeking as well. What would make a special day more so for your mate, your children, your parents, your siblings? Can your home offer them some joy they might not get anywhere else? Giving gifts is part of many holidays, but giving this kind of gift is the essence of holiday itself: holy day, a day to release commonplace concerns and generate gladness from the inside out.

Finally, keep your focus clear: A holiday is about love and lightness. Whether it is a religious, patriotic, or seasonal celebration, or some combination of these, it shouldn't take a holiday to recuperate from one. Cooking from scratch, sewing costumes, making gifts and decorations, and telling every relative you've got that there's plenty of room at your house are great if they appeal to you and if they're feasible at this time in your life. If not, make it easy on yourself by getting to know the deli manager, the nearest thrift store, a catalog, and a good motel. Your children won't suffer if their holidays aren't just like the ones you remember, as long there are some traditions they can look forward to and delight in.

Whatever your style of celebration, do emphasize for your children and yourself the *giving* aspects of the day. As you plan your festivities, think of people you know who are likely to be alone and include them. Remember strangers in some way, too. There are organizations in every community dedicated to serving the poor and disenfranchised. Becoming part of something bigger than yourself can elevate a holiday from wearisome to transformational. Children who are lavished with celebration themselves easily warm to holidays' altruistic underpinnings, and adults who find ways to share the day often feel more like celebrating as a result. Besides, the downside of a holiday is when it fails to live up to anticipations. The safest anticipation is always to be of service.

If you foresee a special day with nothing special for you in it, a day you might have to spend alone, do something about this ahead of time. Make plans to either find a way to serve, celebrate with other people, or give yourself a quiet day for retreat and renewal. If you're new at this, go with the service or the people; they'll keep your attention directed. But if you like time alone and you're not tied to some notion of how a certain day is "supposed to be," you might truly enjoy a day off with only your own companionship.

Plan this day and await it eagerly; you don't want to wake up when it comes and think, "This is awful! I'm alone!" Make it a day for every wish-come-true that you can do for yourself. Read what you like. Eat what you like. Walk. Create. Contemplate. Enjoy immensely every inch of your exquisite environment. If you choose to enjoy a holiday at home by yourself, you've probably already made your home a haven.

## Rites of Passage

Our culture is notoriously devoid of rites of passage, yet we need these to know where we're going in life, just as we need road maps to know where we're going on the highway. Passages happen whether we give them their due or ignore them. It doesn't take pomp and circumstance for a person to grow a year older, earn a degree, become a parent, rise to a higher rank in a company, retire from an occupation, or note the passing of a friend. But with recognition, every such signpost along life's path becomes more meaningful. When acknowledged, the accomplishments carry more pride and the losses less sorrow.

Most of the rites of passage we do observe in Western culture are institutional. The observances are in churches or synagogues, schools or corporations. But the preparation for the baptism, bar mitzvah, graduation, or awards ceremony largely takes place at home. This is where spiritual ideals develop, where students do most of their studying, and where executives get away from the office long enough to come up with the ideas they implement there. I don't suppose anyone has ever received a Nobel Prize or an Academy Award and said, "I wish to thank my kitchen and my den," but these places where we grow toward our potential do factor into the potential that we reach.

Home can also be the site for numerous rites of passage—those as widely recognized as a birthday or anniversary, and those easily disregarded: the day a child learns to tie his sneakers, catch a baseball, or write his name in cursive; the day a friend gets her driver's license, completes a self-defense course, or achieves another year's sobriety in AA. Whatever a person accomplishes takes on a deeper level of reality when others notice, whether there are five hundred "others" in a banquet hall or a handful of well-wishers around a dining room table.

One simple way to congratulate a person for achievement is to serve him or her the "plate of honor." Special ones are sold in gift shops, but any bright plate that stands out from your regular dishes will do, as long as it's not used for other purposes. Children in particular like being singled out for this dinnertime accolade, but adults need it sometimes, too. You can also string a banner announcing "Congratulations!" inside or out, prepare the honoree's favorite entrée or dessert, invite for the occasion one or more of his closest friends, and toast a special person's special day.

Because rites of passage aren't always clear-cut in our society, be on the lookout for important events in other people's lives. Nobody is likely to say, "This really important thing happened. Please notice it and do something to let me know that you did." Instead, listen with your intuition as well as with your ears. "I don't know what I'll do for my birthday since this is the first one since the divorce" can mean, "How would you feel about doing something for my birthday?" I hosted a post-breakup birthday party for a friend once and my "good deed" turned into the most fun I'd had in weeks. I met people I'd never otherwise have known, one of whom was a tireless piano player who accompanied our singing show tunes half the night.

Young people are particularly hungry for rites of passage. In tribal cultures, challenging tasks and elaborate ceremonies initiate boys into manhood. Girls are honored with ritual at the time of their first moon cycle, and instructed in the role their cyclic nature will play in their burgeoning feminine wisdom. Our children need rites of passage just as surely as those in more ritualistically inclined—and some would say healthier—societies. The Jewish bar mitzvah and bat mitzvah come at this important point in young lives, as does confirmation in many Christian churches. Lacking these or in addition to them, look for ways to celebrate youth's progress toward adulthood.

For Katie's thirteenth birthday, her mother, Julie, devised a scrapbook with contributions from every woman who had been important in her daughter's life. Every page contains a picture of Katie with an older friend from the past or present, and a letter or poem from that woman to the girl just entering her teens. The wealth of support, encouragement, and love in that hand-constructed book will be with Katie through the ups and downs of adolescence and for the rest of her life.

Boys need to be brought into their cultural heritage in the presence of a circle of men they trust—fathers, uncles, brothers— who recognize that this boy has become a young man, with the rights and responsibilities that entails. Our identity comes in large part from how we see ourselves reflected in one another's eyes. A boy approaching manhood needs to know from those he would emulate, "We see you differently now."

Being honored is important for all people, both sexes, and every age. When you celebrate a family member or friend in your home, you honor your home as well, and you sanctify its atmosphere with the respect and admiration shown the person in passage. If a home celebration is not in order, do something else for this person. Send a card, plant a tree in his honor, make a video of the special day and send it to him. Add a charm to a bracelet or a photo to an album. Write something from your heart or give a book you think will speak to hers. There are many ways to make a person feel special. Which one you choose isn't nearly as important as doing something at the time that it matters.

Recognize your own rites of passage as well. It's wonderful when someone else knows something is important to you and surprises you with a gift or a gathering at the perfect moment. You can't count on this, though. People are busy, and most of us haven't been trained to be aware of anyone else's red letter days, or even our own. Therefore, be aware of yours. "Celebrate yourself and sing yourself" like Walt Whitman did. Give yourself a gift. Have yourself a frolic. Treat yourself to the company of the most fascinating folks you know.

I once gave myself a splendid birthday party. Instead of inviting the people I see most often and do love dearly (I'll invite *them* another year), I collected around the luncheon table half a dozen women whom I seldom see yet greatly respect. Each guest has an attribute I would hope to increase in my life, and in having them over on my birthday I was symbolically sharing in those qualities. I admire one of these women for her high level of health and fitness, another for her skillful mothering, a third for her literary talent. The others in turn represent to me professional success, poise and refinement, and deep spirituality. It was a magical couple of hours, and I kept the birthday cards on the mantle for the longest time.

Those sentimental souvenirs reminded me that celebration is not simply diversion, it is the meeting point of lives. Wordsworth wrote, "Heaven lies about us in our infancy! ... At length the Man perceives it die away, And fade into light of common day." When we celebrate, we can return to that heavenly childlike state and connect there with people of all ages and varied backgrounds.

I think that one reason children thrive in the presence of grandparents is that most older people are beyond such "common day" concerns as holding down a job and saving for somebody's braces. They can therefore relate with more ease to a child's sense of wonder, and an adolescent's need to go back and forth from the child's world to the adult's at whim and without advance notice. In celebration, though, we can all get in on some ageless magic. We can be children in its merriment and wise in its sacredness. In hosting such celebrations, a house becomes a home, and a home becomes a temple.

# 7
# Sitting

The Buddhists refer to meditation with a charming understatement. They call it "sitting." I like that. It rescues the word "sitting" from the bum rap we've given it as the purview of the couch potato subculture. We tend to think of sitting only as the favored pose of the unmotivated and uninspired, staring at TV screens or playing electronic games until their bodies and minds resemble cornmeal mush that should have been cooked longer. But this indictment of sitting as a whole is unfair. There is a time, to paraphrase Satchel Paige, to "sometimes sit and think—and sometimes just sit."

Nevertheless, we live in a society that applauds activity and distrusts stillness. Examples of this are everywhere. Any exercise instructor will tell you, for instance, that it's customary for a third of the class to leave before the end, before the quiet part, the stretching, the relaxation. They'd rather have sore calves and tight shoulders than allow themselves five minutes of relative idleness.

Instead of teaching our children to take a moment alone of their own volition whenever they need it, we put them in "time out" as a response to inappropriate behavior. We unwittingly instill in them the notion that an interval by ourselves, to take a breather and collect our thoughts, is somehow punishment. Paradoxically, we adults crave time out and rarely take it. It's no wonder so many of us only feel comfortable when we're busy and have such trouble when we attempt to simply *be*.

One of the blessings of home, however, is that it is one place where simply sitting, once you get the knack of it, can yield extraordinary benefits. At home you can be alone in splendid company. This is true whether you live by yourself or claim your solitude by shutting the bathroom door and taping on a "DO NOT DISTURB" sign.

We're all familiar with the kind of sitting we do to wind down: watching TV, reading the paper or the mail, discussing the day's activities. Winding down is necessary. Like the time spent in thought before a chess move, it gives us a chance to regroup before doing the next thing.

But there is also sitting in the Buddhist sense: sitting to, as Walt Whitman put it, "loaf and invite my soul." This "loafing" can consist of classic meditation, a procedure for quieting and calming the mind, or prayer, pensive planning of the day ahead or examination of the one just past, keeping a journal, engaging in thoughtful solitude, or reading something that makes your soul waltz as if its partner were Fred Astaire. For that matter, it can even incorporate centering movement like Tai Chi or yoga (and maybe actual waltzing, too). These aren't "sitting" in the physical sense, but like their more sedentary colleagues, they tell stress to find employment elsewhere.

People who regularly engage in one of these practices grow fond of the place where they do it. "My home is a sanctuary," my friend Loretta said when I told her I was writing this book. "It's a quiet, special, beautiful place. I'm always surprised when other people don't feel this way about their homes." It doesn't surprise me, though, because unlike most "other people," Loretta puts daily quiet time on par with air, water, and food. She reads books for her soul with all the loving attention with which involved parents read storybooks to their children. She underlines in them and highlights in them and makes notes in the margins. She writes in a journal. She meditates without fail every day. Loretta lives in a well-appointed suburban ranch, but I think her home would be "a quiet, special, beautiful place" if she lived in a thin-walled prefab between an airstrip and a stone-crushing plant. Her meditation time creates a peacefulness that can be felt in the air.

Quiet time spent grooming the soul affects a home in two powerful ways. First, it gives a sense of peace to the person who engages in it, and one peaceful person can have a profound effect on a household. It means that at least one person is passing around more serenity than irritation. It initiates a positive ripple effect that can change the dynamics of relationships. This serenity is as noticeable in a regular meditator as developed muscles are in a regular weight lifter. John, a gentleman I know, took up meditation for its stress management benefits after he underwent a quadruple bypass operation. Some months later his wife asked in passing if he had given up meditating. "The truth was," he recalls, "I had quit. What surprised me was that it showed. I went right upstairs and sat on my cushion. I've meditated every day since. That was six years ago."

The second way that quiet, awareness-expanding pursuits benefit a home is that their repeated practice removes tension from the atmosphere itself the way a good air cleaner deals with tobacco smoke. The tranquility and joy that people who meditate realize in their lives can not only be perceived; it can spill over into the place where they meditate, the way a woman's perfume can delicately scent a room through which she's walked. Strangers often enter the home or office of someone who regularly meditates there and say, "It feels so good here." Because it does.

This is not as esoteric as it sounds. There is more unseen activity affecting our lives than what we routinely acknowledge. Television and radio waves, for instance, cannot be seen. Today we take them for granted, but when Marconi initially hypothesized their existence and ways to harness them, he was temporarily incarcerated for insanity. We can't see the activity of thought or the force of love, but we know that these are every bit as real as radio waves. It is on that same unseen vibrational level that the ambience of a home is changed for the better when someone living there takes purposeful silence every day. This is not scientifically validated as are the effects of meditation on human health—there is extensive documentation that daily meditation can play an important role in regulating blood pressure, lowering cholesterol levels, and mitigating anxiety and depression. But I know intuitively that some houses can be depressed, or at least feel as if they are, while others feel warm and happy.

The first gleefully meditative home I experienced belonged to Val, my yoga teacher. The first time I visited her contemporary town house I took a wrong turn on the second floor and instead of walking into a bathroom I entered her *sadhana* room, a room set aside specifically for spiritual practice. It was unfurnished except for a meditation cushion and a simple altar with a candle and a photograph of her spiritual teacher, an Indian holy man named Sathya Sai Baba.

That visit to Val's came during an especially bleak period in my life. My husband, Patrick, had died a few months before and I was grieving. I was also learning to be a single mother, a task which seemed monumental, and working at a job I tolerated but didn't love. When I walked into Val's place, though, I felt much of the grief and confusion I'd been carrying like a knapsack of granite gently lifted from me. And when I wandered into her meditation room, I felt wrapped in comfort. It was as if love had been concentrated there to assure me that, at a time when everything looked all wrong, it would indeed be all right.

I knew at that moment that the most useful thing I could do to help our home shelter my spirit and my daughter's was to do what Val did: go into the silence there every day. I was aware that people had all sorts of ideas on exactly what that should mean— prayer or chanting, reading a certain book, or doing a certain kind of meditation. But it was clear that afternoon in Val's nearly empty second-floor room that the brand of quiet I chose was no more important than my brand of paper clips. What would be important for starting out was doing it: taking the time to be still, recognizing the value of this stillness, and entering into it every day. Exactly what I did in my quiet time wouldn't matter so much, as long as it invited my soul.

I started simply and informally. Every morning, as soon as I knew I was awake and before I remembered to be afraid, I said thank you for ten things that were good in my life at that moment: my daughter, our cats, an idea for a magazine article, a card from a friend. Then I would sit up in bed, pillows propping me up against the headboard, and write in my journal. I wrote how I felt and what I wanted to do that day. Sometimes I wrote down a dream from the night before if it seemed significant. Sometimes I wrote letters to God. Like picking up around the house before the cleaning lady comes, the writing seemed to clear out the surface debris from my mind so my meditation could do the heavy stuff.

I'd had no formal meditation training at that time. Val just told me to watch my breath coming in and going out. I counted the inhalations and exhalations. Inhale, one, exhale, one; inhale, two, exhale, two; inhale, three, exhale, three—up to ten and back again. I did it ten minutes or twenty or thirty, however long it took for me to feel centered and safe and ready for the day.

Most of the time very little happened. I sat there and counted my breaths and watched my mind wandering and thought about what I'd fix for breakfast. But every now and then I went deeper into myself and felt truly at peace. When that happened I knew I would go into the silence the next day and the next until it happened again. It was a juicy carrot on a short stick. I didn't know it then, but in those quiet stretches I was touching my truth.

I recently attended a seminar for speakers. A Dallas consultant named Juanell Teague presented a thought that impressed me as if it had come neon-lit and introduced with a drum roll. She said, "You have to keep going within yourself to find your own truth. If you don't keep discovering new truth, you'll just be rehashing and no one will want to listen to you." This struck me so significantly because she was not addressing a group of avowed spiritual seekers, but rather professional speakers and trainers. These are people who, by and large, make their living helping corporations develop more widgets and helping salespeople sell more of them—not Harvard Divinity by a long shot. If mining for personal truth is necessary in the world of deadlines and bottom lines, think how much more essential it is to sheltering a spirit, nurturing ourselves and our families, and creating harmonious homes.

The process of discovering this truth is a sort of internal one-size-fits-all. Depending on your need and your temperament, it can be intensely spiritual or solidly utilitarian. Pragmatists think of meditative practices as a way to quiet down, and out of that experience of quiet become more productive. Multinational corporations that offer instruction in the Transcendental Meditation technique as an optional company benefit view the process as a cost-effective human development tool. But people who come to meditation with a religious motivation find that it deepens their faith. "I was a committed Christian," a village innkeeper in Scotland once told me, "but after I started to meditate I became a consecrated Christian. It's a purer state—less of me and more of Him."

However an individual approaches it, this is a treasure hunt: for Christianity's "pearl of great price" or Buddhism's "jewel at the center of the lotus." The facets of that jewel could be named peace, patience, mindfulness, healing, courage, creativity, and intuition.

PEACE: People who meditate develop a steadiness, as if they are navigating the seas of life aboard a cruise ship instead of a surfboard. They take life in stride. The small stuff stays small and resources surface for handling the big things, even when we don't have the security of knowing their outcome in advance. Paramahansa Yogananda wrote of this place in consciousness: "At the center of peace I stand. Nothing can harm me here."

We can reach the point at which this realization is so profound that others can feel it simply by being around us. It would be simplistic to say in every case, "If you want a peaceful home, be a peaceful person." There are extreme situations—living with someone who is violent, for instance—where this isn't enough. But for most people in most circumstances, discovering peace within oneself will bring a remarkable degree of peacefulness to a home.

**PATIENCE:** Meditation can be boring. By summoning potential boredom into our lives instead of always avoiding it, we develop patience. Our culture has no respect for boredom, but in Eastern thought it is revered as the mental equivalent of emptiness, the state of receptivity.

A question asked in Zen Buddhism is, "What is the most valuable part of a priceless, antique porcelain bowl?" The answer is its emptiness, its ability to hold rice or potatoes or oranges. Without its functional emptiness, it would lose its identity as "bowl." Without honing our ability to empty our minds of their chatter, we forfeit our opportunity to be fully human. People who sit purposefully every day develop patience with themselves and the rest of us. Trained by listening to silence, they can proficiently listen to words.

**MINDFULNESS:** This means being totally involved in whatever you are doing at the moment. The concept was popularized in the West by Thich Nhat Hanh, the Buddhist monk noted in chapter five for his appreciation of washing dishes. When I read Thich's book *The Miracle of Mindfulness*, a phrase from it took my life from the road it had been on and set it down somewhere else. He wrote that you could wash a teapot with reverence, the same reverence you would feel if you were giving the baby Buddha or Jesus a bath.

That degree of mindfulness comes about largely as a result of daily meditation. This consistent, concentrated focusing of the mind leads to more focus in other aspects of our lives: paying bills, negotiating traffic, giving a presentation, getting through a crisis.

**HEALING:** Meditation and prayer provide a restorative atmosphere for physical and mental healing. They are not a cure per se, but they allow healing to happen, the way a home filled with books does not teach a child to read but provides the raw material for him to become a reader. Deepak Chopra, M.D., writes, "When we experience pure silence in the mind, the body becomes silent also. And in that field of silence, healing is much more efficient."

Healing takes place quietly, unobtrusively. It may be aided physically by medication, surgery, herbs, diet, acupuncture, and a host of therapies appropriate to a particular person and condition. The healing itself, however, is interior, and the greatest healing power is the inner energy of love. We feel love as an emotion by virtue of being human. We come to know it as an energy by going within ourselves to meet it.

**COURAGE:** As a baby boomer, I grew up with fear of nuclear war. Every time I heard a plane fly over, I was afraid it was a Russian bomber and I prayed frantically for it to be TWA instead. I was also afraid that my parents would divorce (they did) and that I would have to get braces on my teeth (I didn't). Either way, I spent a lot of my childhood being afraid.

The fear habit can take hold early, and it doesn't voluntarily release its grip. Fearful people sometimes do courageous things—"whistling in the dark"—but people who meditate tend to develop genuine courage to call on regularly. Sitting produces a broader, clearer view of reality. We get out of the trees of our own situation to see the forest of life as a whole. Fewer things seem frightening. With consistent practice, a sort of cosmic clarity enters one's worldview, and even death provokes more curiosity than fear.

**CREATIVITY:** "We are all richer than we think we are, but we are taught to borrow and beg, and brought up more to make use of what is another's than our own." Emerson wrote this 150 years ago. Today we live even more so in a world of copies, of mass-produced merchandise and repackaged ideas. But as human beings, we carry the touchstone of ingenuity, original thought, and brilliant creativity within us. It is just that the urgencies of life keep most people from going deeply within often enough to tap it. In meditation, we come to know that place where inspiration germinates and impossibility does not exist.

We can use this heightened creative capacity to make an ever more nurturing home for ourselves and those we love. We can use it to deal more cleverly with our personal lives, and we can expand the scope of our creativity into art, invention, and innovation.

**INTUITION:** Intuition is too valuable a faculty to have been ignored by an entire culture, but ours has done its best to disdain this sixth sense. When you start to meditate, however, it does not matter whether you put much stock in intuition or not. Once you've practiced consistently for a while, it will be a more present part of your daily experience. Heightened intuition will join your cognitive and reasoning abilities like someone with a unique background might join a board of directors, adding a fresh perspective.

If you're like most people, you'll ignore your sharpened intuition at first. But after a while, you'll so often hear yourself saying, "I knew I should have done it that way" and "Something just told me I should have left that alone," that you'll pay attention. The "still small voice" makes up in accuracy what it lacks in volume.

# A Smorgasbord of Silence

These are some of the ways that investing a few minutes daily in sitting still can pay handsomely. To cash in, of course, you have to do the sitting. There is a smorgasbord of choices, of ways to go within that suit your temperament and are in keeping with your religious beliefs or lack of them. "You pray like a Christian, meditate like a Hindu, and think like a Buddhist," I was once chided by a friend who is thoroughly ensconced in a single tradition. "Then I can feel at home all over the world," I told him. I have heard since that the mind is most at home in meditation, whatever its form, just the way we are most at home in our own houses.

In yogic teachings, it is recognized that there are a variety of paths that can be taken for spiritual growth. These include study (*jnana yoga*), love and devotion (*bhakti yoga*), and selfless service (*karma yoga*). Each is valid and all can fit into a life in varying proportions. The path of mental clarity through meditation, however, is known as *raja yoga,* the kingly path, a straight, precise, definite road to peace and fulfillment.

The three easiest ways to meditate are using the *breath,* a *mantra,* and *contemplation.* Human beings have long associated breath and spirit. One definition of the word "inspiration" is "the drawing of air into the lungs." Another is "a divine influence or action on a person." To meditate using breath as the focus, you merely observe your own breathing: counting each breath as I learned from Val, or just watching your inhalations and exhalations come and go, feeling the air touch your nostrils and leave again. Classic Buddhist meditation, taught in many places throughout the world as *Vipassana* (Insight) Meditation, relies on this simple but profound technique.

A mantra is a word or sound or phrase used in conjunction

with steady breathing as a focal point for the mind. A mantra can have rational meaning or be only a sound vibration. *Om*, the sacred sound in Indian tradition, can be chanted aloud or repeated silently. Holding in mind a phrase such as "God is love" or "I am peace" works, too. Inhale on "God is" or "I am" and exhale on "love" or "peace."

Contemplation, also known as contemplative prayer, is a form of meditation long practiced in the West. To do this, become still with a few deep breaths and afterward read a prayer or a page or a paragraph of spiritual literature. Then sit quietly and contemplate the meaning of what you have read. Play the words over in your mind. You might silently recite a select phrase to the rhythm of your breathing. In contemplation, you don't stop with thinking about what you've read; you allow its meaning to become a part of you, an operational component of your life. This doesn't happen in a day or a week, but like any skill, it develops over time. Keep at it.

Meditation is said to be more effective if you sit comfortably with your back straight, either cross-legged on the floor or on a cushion, or in a chair with your two feet on the floor. Your hands can rest in your lap or on the chair arms, palms up if that's comfortable. Your body may get restless, but it will calm down after a few sessions. Many people find that doing a few yoga postures or basic stretching exercises prior to meditation prepares the body to sit.

The mind, however, is more challenging. Much of the time, it is apt to be everywhere but with you. Saint Francis compared our mobile thoughts to flying birds. He said that it was harmless to watch them fly, but not to let them "make a nest in your hair." In other words, just observe your mind and bring it gently back to your breath or your mantra or the subject of your contemplation.

It's a misconception to think that the meditative state is total emptiness. That's not meditation, it's a coma. In meditation, thoughts will come and go; you neither encourage them to stay nor force them out.

Sometimes, innovative ideas and solutions to problems will come to you during meditation. More practically, you may remember at this time something you need to do during the day: "Your suit is ready at the cleaners. Pick up a loaf of bread at the store." One school of thought says you should ignore all this and stay with your breath. I choose to acknowledge any apparently useful thought that surfaces, make a mental note of it, and then return to my conscious breathing.

The amount of time you spend is up to you. Ten minutes seems to be the minimum to reap any benefits from sitting. Those who meditate for an hour say it helps them get more accomplished in the remaining twenty-three. Proponents of Transcendental Meditation, a specialized mantra technique, recommend twenty minutes of meditation twice a day. More than five hundred scientific journal articles attest to the value of the TM technique in stress management and health improvement.

However you devise your quiet time, do it every day. If you miss a day, don't miss the next one. Like exercise or learning to play an instrument or to speak another language, this takes discipline—not because it's unpleasant, just because it's new. Help yourself get into the habit every way you can:

*Make the time for meditation (or prayer or journal-writing or whatever you choose to do) rather than expecting to find the time.* What will this require in your life? For many people, it means getting up half an hour earlier or staying up a bit later at night.

Whatever it takes, the time you give to meditation will return to you in the form of a more productive life.

*Write "Meditate" at the top of your planning calendar every day for a month.* Check it off when you've done it as if it were a report due or a haircut appointment.

*Light a candle as soon as you get up in the morning.* When you come back from the bathroom, the lit candle will remind you to sit for a few minutes.

*Take a meditation class.* Places to look for these include hospitals, holistic health centers, yoga centers, churches and temples, and adult education programs. You'll learn helpful techniques and meet other people who value quiet time. (If you wish to learn Transcendental Meditation [TM], look in your local White Pages.)

*Make a commitment to a friend that you will have quiet time regularly for thirty days.* Check in with this person daily during the commitment period.

*Set reasonable goals.* Give each sitting as much time as you reasonably can. Unless you are doing TM or another practice with a specified time recommendation, the optimal amount of time to spend is the time you are honestly willing to spend. Consistency is the important thing: You're building a habit, not training for a marathon.

*Choose about the same time every day for your inner work.* The mind gets used to meditating on schedule and is more compliant when the schedule is predictable. Some people say that certain times of day are especially suited for meditation. I've heard, for instance, that two and a half hours before sunrise is ideal, but that is a time of day I have rarely witnessed, much less spent meditating. Nevertheless, there is something to be said for taking quiet time when it is truly quiet, early in the morning or late at night, depending upon your schedule and your body rhythms. TM suggests morning meditation and another session in the afternoon or early evening to balance the day's activity with reliable periods of the deep rest that meditation affords.

*Consider others' feelings.* If you are the only person in your house who meditates, it's good to do it when everyone else is sleeping or away. If you're a parent, you know how this works. It always seems that the minute you pick up the phone, kids who were absorbed in play just a moment before suddenly require your immediate attention. Meditation elicits a similar response, and not just from children.

A person sitting with her eyes closed appears to be committing the mortal sin of our time: nonperformance. Interrupting this does not seem rude. For those unused to meditation, it doesn't look like there's anything to interrupt. Also, when you're meditating and those around you aren't, you appear to be shutting people out, and they don't like it. Unless you can interest your partner or another family member in meditating with you, it's better to keep a low profile and let the positive changes in you affect everyone else in subtle ways.

*Practice with another person when possible.* If you live with someone who wants to share quiet time with you, you are fortunate indeed. When two people meditate together, the power seems to intensify by a factor greater than the obvious one plus one. The Christian view of this is Jesus' saying, "For where two or three are gathered together in my name, there am I in the midst of them." I learned about this firsthand when my friend Jean house-sat in my neighborhood for a few months. She came over in the morning, maybe four days out of every seven, and we meditated together. We seemed to reach that place of deep rest and peacefulness more quickly when two of us were going there together.

*Establish a meditation group.* Those "good vibrations" your own meditation will give your home are intensified if it becomes a center for group practice. Hosting a weekly group also provides unparalleled impetus for staying faithful to your personal quiet time. Cate and Cor, a couple I know, started a Friday evening meditation group in their Manhattan apartment. "After a few months," Cate says, "we just knew that nothing harmful could happen in that apartment. We had created sacred space out of normal, everyday space—normal, noisy New York space at that—and we hadn't even set out to do it."

*Have a specific place for meditation, ideally one that is free of major distractions.* A *sadhana* room like Val's may be out of the question, but a special chair or earmarked corner probably isn't. I still meditate in my bedroom. Maybe that's why it's my favorite room in the house.

Devising a meditation site that encourages your practice should be a pleasure, because the primary prerequisite for this place is that *you* like it. It should also be clean and uncluttered, the way you want your mind to become as a result of your sitting. Think first of where you will take your quiet time. Do you want to meditate in your bedroom? The living room? How public a spot do you want this to be? How elaborate do you want to make it? Are there sensibilities of other family members to take into account?

You may wish to construct a small altar for your practice. This is not to everyone's taste. My literary agent, Patti Breitman, supports her belief in simplicity with an "invisible altar," a place of emptiness in the midst of an active life. "Our houses are so full," she says, "that a meditation place can be the space we set aside for having nothing." For me, having an altar I can see is a reminder of my inner life every time I glimpse it. And when I awaken in the morning it is there to remind me to schedule in my time apart. My small altar is so meaningful to me that I bring a picture of it along when I travel. I put the photo on a hotel nightstand and I'm ready for meditation wherever I am.

My altar is a little tag sale table, 12 x 24 inches, with several objects on it that are significant to me. On top is an embroidered runner stitched by Karma Lhadon, the Tibetan refugee child we sponsor in Nepal. It reminds me of all the Tibetans I know, and how their mighty faith, vast tolerance, and infectious humor have intensified my spiritual life. Atop the runner are a votive candle and a rose-glazed incense burner holding sticks of frankincense. I love the ritual of the Catholic Mass, so candlelight and frankincense represent holiness to me.

Also on my altar is a sixteenth-century bronze Buddha statue that belonged to my husband and invariably reminds me of the story of the Buddha's enlightenment. After years of searching for truth in teachers and philosophies and self-denial, this erstwhile prince sat beneath a tree to meditate, to find the truth within himself. After forty days he arose a different man. People asked, "Are you God?" He said, "No. I am awake." The statue personifies for me the meditation process and its role in a soul's awakening.

My other altar object is a small red rock I picked up along the Lake Michigan shore in a remote part of Wisconsin. Over the years this rock has resided on windowsills and in desk drawers. I often didn't know where it was, but it always turned up somewhere. During this time, I lost a passport and a diary and a diamond ring, but I still have that rock. I finally put it on my altar where it brings a bit of the natural world to my spiritual life. Of course, you can meditate outside and get your nature direct. Some Native Americans say that prayer is heard by the Great Spirit only when the feet of the person praying touch the earth.

## A Place of Prayer

With this mention of prayer, it is important to note that personal prayer, as opposed to formal meditation or meditation alone, can take you into the silence as well. Although meditation asks for no belief in anything beyond the likelihood of your next breath, prayer is for those whose reality includes an accessible Higher Power. Even those who are far from certain about the existence or character of such a Power can feel the desire to pray. An endearing example of a prayer from someone in this situation is included in Jerrold Mundis's book *Earn What You Deserve*: "In the unlikely event that there is any motivating force in the universe, in the improbability that it is even remotely aware that the species exists, and in the near impossibility that it has in any way contributed to anything that is good in my life—I am appreciative."

For some people, prayer and meditation go hand in hand—"talking to God, then letting God answer." There is no wrong way to pray since, as Mark Twain put it, "You cannot pray a lie." Sometimes it's reassuring to simply say prayers learned in childhood or read those written by other people. These can imprint on our consciousness so the ones we most admire can be with us all the time.

I sometimes wake up and find my mind reciting the Serenity Prayer:

"God grant me the serenity to accept the things I cannot change, the courage to change the things I can, and the wisdom to know the difference." Other mornings I awaken with James Dillet Freeman's prayer: "The light of God surrounds me. The love of God enfolds me. The power of God protects me. The presence of God watches over me. Wherever I am, God is." I have these prayers and a score of others stored in my memory like extra blankets for a cold night.

Of course, prayer doesn't have to be formal, written down and memorized, or have a nice rhythm to it. In its most personal and spontaneous expression, prayer responds to life. It's usually some version of "Help!" You can read a lot about how best to say this: humbly, faithfully, beseechingly, or affirmatively, i.e., "God helps me," instead of, "God, help me." (This way, the logic goes, you're convincing yourself of the reality that help is indeed available.) My hunch is that if a prayer comes from the heart, the words don't matter.

The laboratory researchers who have looked at prayer from a scientific perspective have found that those prayers that get the desired results seem to come from people who believe, first, in the power of prayer and, second, in their own worthiness to have one answered. Knowing what prayer promises and what it doesn't is also necessary. When I was wrestling with this, Duke Tufty, a spiritual teacher whose opinions I respect, told me that all the scriptures of the world promise that prayers are answered. The answers, however, aren't winning lottery numbers and marriages to movie stars. Although these could fulfill secondary longings, prayer deals with primary needs, those that all human beings share: the need for inner peace, well-being, and freedom from fear so we can deal with whatever circumstances confront us.

This, I think, is mature prayer to encourage an expanding spirit and foster a tranquil heart. It can be a companion as well as a comfort. In talking with my friends Robert and Janet Ellsworth, coauthors of *Prayers That Work*, Robert said, "Since we talk to ourselves all the time anyway, we might as well talk to a responsive, friendly universe." So talk. Ask for yourself and for others. Offer prayers of praise and prayers of gratitude. Share your thoughts with a Higher Power, and uplift your way of thinking with affirmative statements and positive images. Your soul will benefit, and so will your home.

## No-Obligation Guarantee

The only way to know whether taking a soul break at home every day will be of benefit to you is to try living both with it and without it. As an experiment, meditate fifteen of the next thirty days. (I'm using "meditate" to apply to all spiritual practice.)

Keep track of each day, and every evening write a brief summary of how the day went: "Even though I was out late last night, I felt good today and got a lot accomplished," or "I was so self-possessed in the midst of my boss's outburst, she actually apologized before lunch," or "I was snappy with everybody; I thought I'd lost my wallet (it turned out to be in my coat pocket), and I'm glad this day is over." My guarantee to you is this: If you don't see a strong connection between "good days" when you meditate and "bad days" when you don't, you can feel secure in the knowledge that you are unique.

In addition to the benefits of formal, daily sitting, you will be able—once you've done it for a while—to tap that peaceful place within you on short notice. A couple of minutes away from a tense situation to do some focused breathing can be a godsend. If that isn't possible, two deep inhalations and exhalations are enough to trigger relaxation in the mind and body. Accompanying these with silent statements of "I am calm," can shift you into a renewed state of mind with remarkable efficiency.

As you become used to taking a block or two of time each day for the benefit of your interior being, you will naturally take other moments as the need arises. You will grow accustomed to claiming as your right the time and solitude necessary to oversee a spiritual life. It will be a priority. *You* will be a priority.

Even sitting in its most mundane sense—the winding down referred to early in the chapter—will take on another dimension. You will give yourself the grace to linger over dinner, whether you have guests or not. You will allow yourself to listen to your favorite music, even when you aren't calculating your budget or making a grocery list at the same time. You will hand yourself an invisible permission slip to, every now and then, simply sit and enjoy your home. At times when you are not tidying it or repairing it or tending to someone's needs in it, you will remember to luxuriate in the place where you live.

If this puts your work ethic on red alert, remind yourself that the work of the soul doesn't always look like much from the outside. The spirituality of everyday life includes listening to another person without a time allotment, watching the seasons change outside your windows, and being with your own musings without chiding yourself for inactivity. It includes knowing that any time spent by conscious choice is never wasted.

Home is the place to realize this. If you just sat in school, you were goofing off. If you just sit at the office, you're daydreaming on company time. But if you just sit at home, you can do it barefoot or in your bathrobe, or while you eat a chocolate sandwich cookie, middle first. And you can sense the sweetness of this finest place on earth.

# 8
# Comforts

In the pre-video days of my childhood, I had the distinction of seeing a single motion picture thirteen times: *Auntie Mame*, with Rosalind Russell playing the avant-garde flapper-era guardian of an orphaned nephew. "Life is a banquet," Mame said, "and most poor suckers are starving to death." I was imprinted by that movie with the admonition to fill my plate. That's what comforts are, bountiful helpings from life's banquet table. These aren't confined to comfort in the physical sense; they include everything that gives you unmitigated joy.

The first thing you notice in people who value their own comforts is that they do not abide compromise, downgrading, or generic substitution of something that is personally significant. For instance, since I write, pens are important to me. There is one kind of pen I dearly love to work with; it floats across the page in a line so thin I feel as if I'm drafting a paragraph the way an architect drafts a ceiling angle.

I don't always remember how vital this comfort is, though. Recently, I bought a box of a different model, same brand, to save a few dollars. Now every time I write with one of those second-choice pens I notice the difference. Respecting comforts is not the same as being extravagant. I buy drugstore pantyhose and my car has reached adolescence, but I need my special pens, because the pleasure I get from the way they feel spills out onto the paper.

I think most of us look at personal delights as somewhere between minimally important and borderline immoral. We like them, but we're not sure we ought to. We seldom give them a high priority when other demands are competing for our attention. Nevertheless, the soul feeds on simple joys and withers without them.

Comforts are highly individual. Most often it *is* more blessed to give than receive, and we derive great comfort from doing something for someone else. But treating yourself to something engaging has merit, too. When you do it frequently enough, you become the sort of person who attracts good into your life.

It happens like this: Let's say you like coffee. You appreciate it enough to order the beans from a cooperative in Guatemala, grind them yourself, and brew up a fragrant pot every morning. Now let's imagine you're out of town and want some coffee. You won't stop at a fast food place for a Styrofoam cup of something remotely similar to what you have at home. No. You'll seek out a charming coffee bar in the art district, discover a blend you've never tried before, and learn from the university paper on the table that there's a chamber music concert tonight. You go. You sit next to a friendly couple who knew your old violin teacher. Now you see them whenever you're in their city—if only for a cup of coffee.

If that sounds like a foolish little story and nothing like that ever happens to you, look at yourself in relation to those things that lift your spirits like a helium balloon. How often do you give yourself something that touches you at that exquisite emotional point just between laughter and tears? Or how often do you just have fun for the heck of it? There are an unlimited number of ways to feel on top of the world. I asked twenty-five people about at-home comforts and got twenty-five responses:

> *"Looking through my photo albums."*
> *"Sleeping in."*
> *"Reading."*
> *"A fire in the fireplace."*
> *"It's whenever my teenage son wants to talk. I drop anything then because I know we won't be having these talks forever."*

For me one night it was listening to the score of *The Phantom of the Opera*. I'd checked out the CD from the library and felt euphoric hearing music that hadn't cost me a dime.

> *"Having friends over."*
> *"Our king-size bed when it attracts both kids, a couple of cats, Scattergories or Pictionary, and a big bowl of popcorn."*
> *"Stupid sitcoms."*
> *"Early mornings: When I come back from my run, the sun is just coming up and everyone is still asleep. I have about half an hour to plan my day and get a handle on things."*
> *"When my wife and I trade massages."*

If we don't oblige them with a touch of ecstasy every so often, our inner selves nag at us. Have you heard of wish-fulfillment dreams? When our inner being is after something and we don't respond, it can try to get through to us in dreams. For example, I love speaking French and I wish I spoke it better than I do. It was one of those "some day I'll get around to it" things. Then one night I dreamed that I was in France at a fabulous restaurant where I swear I could smell the tarragon and the table wine. But in the dream I couldn't speak enough French to order a meal.

The next day I put my Berlitz tapes in the car; now I can parlay driving into *parlez français*. If my unconscious wants something enough to ask for it in the middle of the night, it's not a request I can deny. What have you been dreaming while you sleep? What are your dreams in the daytime?

> *"I like to buy a* Vogue *magazine and give myself two hours in bed to read it."*

> *"Getting home and knowing my dog will be there."*

> *"Walking on my treadmill while I watch* Oprah.*"*

> *"Talking on the phone with a friend who lives far away."*

> *"The forty-five minutes I get in the evenings when my husband gives our son his bath and reads to him. Sometimes I do absolutely nothing during those forty-five minutes, but I think they ensure my sanity."*

People who know how to cater to their soul needs—their genuine comforts—seem to live charmed lives. They set out to please themselves and the universe cooperates. They're in the right place at the right time. They know the right people. Events happen in their lives that seem almost magical. Beneficial coincidences are commonplace. My friend Rita is like that. She had been out of a job for quite a while when she received an invitation to rendezvous with a traveling friend in Europe. She figured she had already applied for every job in her field in Chicago, so she bought a plane ticket with her last unemployment check. After a postcard-perfect time, she returned refreshed and confident and landed a job a week later. Rita knows how to live.

People who easily give themselves comforts, like Rita, are the ones we say have style. They provide themselves with the very best of those few material things that they need to be the best, and those are the ones we notice. Sometimes these people are rich. Other times they just live as if they are—not by going into debt, but by giving themselves those things, even cheap or free, that make them feel good.

> *"Watching the rabbits and chipmunks in my yard."*
>
> *"Sunday mornings with the* Times *and some very gooey, very fattening, very delectable pastry."*
>
> *"Tending the garden."*
>
> *"Wearing old clothes, like the sweats and wool clogs I clomp around in."*
>
> *"Singing in the shower."*

Comforts aren't confined to home, of course, but at-home comforts have an advantage in being readily available and, for the most part, already paid for. I recently rode with a taxi driver who told me that driving was a second job so he could pay off debts. His strategy for financial independence? "I don't go anywhere and I don't do anything." I asked if this spartan lifestyle was difficult. "Oh, no," he said. "I've never been happier." He explained how he had become an excellent cook (I got his recipe for marinara sauce), was playing trumpet for the first time since high school, and refurnishing much of his house by refinishing attic heirlooms. Going "nowhere" and doing "nothing" can lead to a high-quality life.

> *"Living without the technology I coexist with at the office: At home I don't have a PC or a TV, and my phone's got a dial."*
>
> *"Sitting on the porch swing in the summer."*

*"Fixing things. Working on the house. I didn't build it, but I'm contributing to it."*

*"Watching movies."*

*"Falling asleep at night with my husband's arms around me."*

Be person number twenty-six in the comfort survey. What do you do at home to feel comfortable and cared for? Even comforts that look like petty indulgences have a place in every home and every life. They're physical rewards and emotional refuelers. You're happier and healthier and nicer to other people when you get them.

Your soul responds to these treats the way a student does to an A+. That's because this life we're living is school, school for the soul. When you've lived long enough you come to see that every challenge that looks overwhelming is just life, in its role as teacher, putting an assignment on the board. If life can give the tests it does, it ought to have a drawer full of gold stars, too.

By going within yourself to discover what comforts you, you learn a lot about yourself. Some people are laser-focused: One aspect of life brings them so much satisfaction that they require little else. Their key comfort and what they do for a living may be related, or they may be content with some seemingly inconsequential job because their substance comes from something else, from some passion that doesn't need a paycheck attached. These people are often highly creative—so gifted in, for example, music that music in various forms is virtually the only comfort they need.

More of us, however, have myriad parts to ourselves that don't necessarily line up like ducks in a row. My divergent leanings more often resemble a rambunctious litter of pups than an orderly parade of ducklings. This disturbed me in my overly serious youth when I tried to eradicate from my personality the parts that didn't fit with the rest of me, or with my image of myself. One of my first mentors interrupted this self-abridgement process when she said: "If you want to sparkle like a diamond, you need all your facets. Instead of destroying them, you ought to be polishing them." We polish our facets by frequent exposure to what delights us.

The activities we've explored in this book up to now can be quite comforting in themselves: creating a physical environment that pleases all your senses, finding peace and renewal in quiet time, and breaking free from clutter or credit or whatever other complication might have weighed you down. It's a comfort to shop for food in congenial surroundings and prepare one simple, perfect dish. It even feels good to clean your house when you do it as a spiritual exercise. A special celebration when everything goes right, or at least when everything worth remembering goes right, becomes a cherished keepsake of the heart. And there are hundreds of other comforts you can customize at home and take with you wherever you go.

For my parting gift to you as these chapters wind to a close, I want to let you in on a few of my favorite comforts. Some, like safety and daily routine, can benefit anyone. Others may suit you or not, but if they remind you of comforts you can give yourself, they've served their purpose.

## The Comfort of Daily Routine

Routine isn't a glamorous word, but having one can be a comfort of the highest order. Waking up with some certainty of what comes next, some sense of regularity amid a day's inevitable surprises, holds within it peace and stability.

Robert Fulghum writes insightfully of daily routine in his

essay "Pay Attention," in the anthology *Handbook for the Soul*. He says: "Certain activities, structures, and ritual patterns have become woven into the fabric of my daily life because they have been so consistently useful to me—because they nourish my soul." It's not that he never deviates, "But if I stick to my routine regularly four days out of seven, my life goes well."

That's about right for anybody. The protocols themselves are unique to each individual, but the benefit of keeping to them a little more than half the time seems to be the minimum for benefitting from a personally established daily routine.

Think about your day, starting with when you get up. Do you awaken around the same time every morning? What habits typically punctuate this early part of your day? If you work outside your home, how do you get to work? Do you walk or drive or carpool or take a bus or a train? Do you enjoy your travel time? Could you do something to enjoy it more? Do brief personal rituals make their way into your workday—a walk after lunch maybe, or a call to your children when they get home from school? Is there time for yourself late in the day, a few minutes for personal reflection and shifting from your work attitude to your home self? What do you do to make dinner special? How do you spend your evenings? How do you prepare to retire at night?

Go over these questions carefully and give some thought to answering each one. They're not idle inquiries; your answers will tell you if your daily routine is nourishing your soul and, surprisingly perhaps, your body. Although I always felt a certain comfort in having some similarity day to day, it wasn't until I indulged myself in a transformative health spa experience that I learned how necessary routine can be. I went to the Raj in Fairfield, Iowa, where the teachings and treatments are based on Ayurveda, an ancient Indian system of preventive health care. Ayurveda proposes that, in addition to meditation, a good diet, proper physical activity and the like, high-level health and a balanced life depend upon *dinacharya*, Sanskrit for daily routine. The rationale is that as natural beings, we live in greatest health and joy when we are in tune with nature. Ideally, this means rising when the sun does, eating at regular mealtimes and sitting quietly for a few minutes afterward, exercising around the same time each day, going to bed by 10:00 or 10:30, and generally giving our bodies and minds a predictable schedule in keeping with basic physiological and ecological parameters.

Routine in the morning is most essential to me. I know that what I set out to do between 6:00 and 8:00 A.M. is likely to be accomplished without interruption. After that, I never know. Even making the bed is a pleasant morning ritual. I never mastered the skill as a child; beds always seemed wider than the spread of my arms. At summer camp, my lumpy cot kept our cabin from getting the tidiness award. But now I can make a bed and once I do, I know that a new day is beginning in earnest.

I cherish the morning's early hours, when I do yoga postures and meditate and give myself a massage with warm sesame oil, an Ayurvedic suggestion for both calming the nervous system and building resistance to disease. After my shower and making breakfast, the rest of the world starts to have its say about what I'll do and where I'll be, but at least I can bank on two hours of dependable sameness.

Your daily routine paints a portrait of your life. Look it over again. What hours are out of your hands? Where can you have more input? Can you establish a morning routine or an evening one, or even a Saturday or Sunday routine that you can count on?

The idea is not to cling rigidly to the established pattern, but rather to have a pattern you'll want to return to when you've been away from it. Be sure your routine is supportive of your priorities and that it allows you the pleasures that for you make life worthwhile. If it doesn't, the routine is a rut. If it does, it's a comfort.

## The Comfort of the Bath

I knew I would buy my house the minute I saw the bathtub. It's old and huge and sits on feet. Bathtubs of that vintage were shaped to conform to the human spine. Whoever designed those bathtubs knew that you don't take a bath just to get clean. You take a bath to get away from the world, to mull things over, to relax completely, and send tension down the drain.

To me, a hot bath is luxury beyond description. It deserves to be treated as such. Each one can be an event. Block out time for it on your appointment calendar. Decide what you want from this bath: Do you want to pamper yourself? Calm down after a hectic day? Prepare for a special evening? Think through a knotty problem? Soothe aching muscles or stiff joints? Orchestrate your bath accordingly. It doesn't have be complicated: A pampering bath may mean you put on a facial masque and a calming one may mean you play your tape of Gregorian chants. It doesn't take complex measures for your body and psyche to respond.

If your bathtub isn't as comfortable as mine, get one of those bath pillows with suction cups so you can lean back and really relax. (They also come covered in terry cloth if you don't like the feel of plastic.) And by all means pour stuff in the water. What you put in doesn't matter nearly as much as the fact that you cared enough about yourself to take a bath in something more elaborate than naked water.

There are a lot of high-quality products on the market, many of them hypoallergenic for the sensitive. Some people like bubbles. Some like oil. I like salts. Even the phrase is nice: bath salts. It elicits images of an old-time apothecary filled with curious elixirs for whatever ails you. I like exotic bath salts that claim to come from the Dead Sea and basic ones that claim to be good for rheumatism. Those with aromatherapeutic properties—delectable smells that are supposed to make a person feel calm, energetic, or ripe for falling in love—add a scented dimension.

How's your soap? I'm not a collector—collections remind me of people stockpiling canned goods for the apocalypse. But if I were to collect something, it would be soap. The nice ones are like lovely little sculptures—squares and ovals and octagons. There are shiny ones in vivid colors, roughly textured ones full of almonds and oatmeal, soft green ones with olive oil, and chunky white ones made of coconut. These cost little more than grocery store soap, but they make taking a bath seem more sumptuous and less utilitarian.

Candles are exquisite to bathe by. You know what candlelight does to soften and beautify a face. It does the same thing for a bathroom, fading away the room's imperfections and making of it a comforting refuge. Candlelight is calming. It's as if anxiety is absorbed by the flame. You can even match your candles' scent to your soap and your bath salts. (I'm lucky to come up with two matching towels, much less matching soap and candles, but the room smells great just the same.)

And do take your time. There should be some accepted understanding among humans that jumping out of the tub for anything short of an emergency is just not done. Bathing, when respectfully approached, puts you in a blissful, netherworld state. It's jarring to rush out of that state and plunge headlong into this one. You don't jump up from meditation to mow the lawn. You don't jump up from making love to patch the roof. You ease out of profound experiences, so ease out of the tub into a soft, ample towel. (If you want to do something totally endearing for someone, provide him or her with warmed towels after a bath.)

Unless you need to dress immediately, spend some time in a terry cloth robe that's at least one size too big for you. Time spent in your robe is transitional, between the time of the bath and the next indicated task. The difference between a four-star hotel and a five-star hotel is that the five-star ones provide their guests with terry cloth robes. There is no reason that any of us can't take a five-star bath right at home.

## The Comfort of Words

My seventh grade teacher, Mrs. Buckley, made the class memorize poems until we were a human anthology. Everyone griped about it, but even then I had a hunch she was giving me something I could cash in later, like a U.S. Savings Bond. Some years after that, a spiritual director taught me that it was critical to fill my mind with lofty ideas, passages of scripture and poetry, and words of inspiration and uplift. He said that in the ebb and flow of life, I would at times be sad or lonely or confused. In such times, those words— even the ones I thought I'd forgotten—would be there for me like an understanding friend who always has the right thing to say. Thanks to my seventh grade teacher, I'd already experienced this and knew that it was true.

It is at home where we're most likely to fill our minds with words of beauty, faith, honor, and wonder. Memorization such as Mrs. Buckley demanded of her students is a dying art, but it can be revived in the life of anyone who wants it. If a phrase touches your heart, stick it on your refrigerator, your telephone, or your mirror. Live with it a while and let it become part of you. Have ready access to books containing the words you want to make your own. Bring a proverb or pithy saying to dinner to share with your children. Put inspirational books in the bathroom where you're most apt to read them. Even a thought-for-the-day calendar or a recorded Dial-an-Inspiration might tell you just what you need to hear.

At home you can be somewhat choosy about the information you absorb. You can decide here, to a greater extent than at the office or the mall, what you'll read, what you'll take in via radio and television, and the people with whom you'll talk. The words and images that come from all these sources take up residence inside you. You have the power to focus on those the old hymn calls "wonderful words of life." File them away in your mind or in your journal—words that are touching, words that are funny, words that are so beautiful they make the hairs on your arms stand up. They'll be there for you when you need them most.

Moreover, you can make a gift of your own words to those you live with. The Buddhists say, "Be mindful of your words, for they can cause both joy and pain." This mindfulness can seem more like a moral exercise than a comfort, but it saves you from the discomfort of wishing you could eat a sentence or two. Let your home be a safe haven from hurtful words and a sure source of those that offer hope and assurance.

## The Comfort of Creativity

There is tremendous joy in making something, in bringing into being an object or a plan or an experience that germinated deep within you. Some people are able to put their creative side to use in their jobs, but for all of us home can be a creative center. It invites enterprising pursuits from crafts, cooking, and carpentry to raising violets and raising children. Simply keeping house or keeping a journal, giving a party or giving a back rub, can be home-based creativity at its best.

I was at a pottery sale and heard one of the potters talking about his house. "The studio space sold me on the place," he said. "There was just no more looking after that." This kind of collaboration of home and art shelters the spirit in a dynamic, productive way, but it needn't be confined to artists in the traditional sense. Any time we usher something from imagination into form, we're creating.

A friend of mine commented to her young daughter that it will be interesting to see what fields the child will pursue, since she has a variety of talents. "I know," the little girl responded solemnly. "It's such a burden." The truth is, we're all "burdened" with creativity. When we exercise this capacity, we're doing the most amazing thing a human being can. We're doing what God does.

When I was in third grade catechism in Catholic school, the nun asked the question, "How did God create the world?" The right answer—in catechism class, there was always one specific, right answer—was, "He made it from Himself because there was nothing else." I think we create from ourselves, too. Our tools might be a guitar or a camera, a dancer's body, or pen and ink, but what we create comes from inside us, from our soul-selves, where we have access to boundless creativity.

How do you create? What inventive activity gives you the most exhilaration? How much creativity are you able to employ in your job? How much do you fit in at home? Where do you rank creative pursuits on your list of priorities? Have you made a place in your house or apartment to accommodate your creative side?

Having such a place is important in a practical way since creative pursuits aren't often neat. They don't take well to physical confinement. Their side effects include wood shavings, fabric scraps, dirty brushes, dirty dishes, discarded papers, and the neglect of more mundane occupations. If we expect creativity to flourish in our homes, we need to allow for its consequences.

Half the disarray in children's rooms is creative overflow— scraps of construction paper, stray scissors, uncorked glue, and watercolor water in that awful shade of brown-tinged purple. These rooms are anathema to outsiders but paradise to a young artist. Alexander Pope said, "Order is heaven's first law," but I think order is heaven's second law. Creativity had to come first so there could be something to put in order.

Few adults maintain the uninhibited creativity of children, but that capacity isn't lost; it's just buried amid grown-up complexities. We uncover it whenever we have the courage to express ourselves. Frequent contact with beauty also primes the creative pump. It seems to me that much of what we create is recycled beauty that grows out of exposure to nature and the creations of other people. At that pottery sale, I was thinking, "I wonder if this teapot is reinterpreted Mozart." Maybe this chapter is a reworked teapot, glazed in blue with a bamboo handle.

## The Comfort of Tea

I take great pleasure in tea. This is a legacy from the year I lived in London just after high school. My mother said to live in a good neighborhood, even if it meant taking a one-room flat. It did. My

"kitchen" was a cupboard with a small oven/hot plate combination, no fridge, and sorely limited storage space. I stocked my single shelf with two tins of tea—peachy Oolong and bergamot-
scented Earl Grey—a box of sugar cubes, and a couple of tins of
condensed milk. I figured I was ready, even if Her Majesty
stopped by.

It was in England that I learned the rites of tea: using a spoon-
ful for each person and an extra one for the pot, warming the
teapot with hot water first, then pouring freshly boiled water over
the tea, letting it steep five minutes, and pouring it out through a
strainer. In the years since, caffeine and I have generally parted
company, so today I prefer herbal teas but stick to the ritual just
the same. My favorite tea at this point is a heady blend of exotic
spices sold under the brand name "Yogi Tea." It is customarily
served with milk or soy milk and honey or raw sugar. The result is
creamy and comforting, whether hot or over ice.

I use tea bags for breakfast or when I just want a quick cup of
tea. That's fine, but it doesn't go nearly as far on the comfort scale
as tea that is ceremonially prepared. The process takes on a soul-
fulness as you go through the motions of warming the pot and letting the tea infuse while it's warmly dressed in a tea cozy. (How
can you not love something called a cozy?) People appreciate
being served tea thus made. For women, it probably harkens back
to the tea party days of childhood when we lovingly poured for
dolls and teddy bears. For both sexes, though, there's an ambience
to a pot of tea that seems to help people relax. Sipping a really
good cup of tea makes a guest feel welcome and at home.

Having people over "for tea" is a disarming way to entertain
friends without the work of making a full meal. This would never
have occurred to me until my daughter's friend Ashley planned an

afternoon tea for her birthday party. She *really* had a tea: The girls wore dresses and gloves, drank from china cups, and ate scones and wee cucumber sandwiches (crusts removed, of course). My teas are less highbrow than that. The tea is served in mugs and the sandwiches are likely to be peanut butter, but the overall tone is there: an afternoon gathering with light refreshments so the focus is on the people instead of on the food.

During the holiday season, an afternoon tea can be a welcome break from evening commitments; it's also an actual reason for baking all those angel-shaped cookies. In the summer, move a tea outdoors. And any time of year, a private tea for one special person is a captivating gift. Surprise a child after school with a pretty tea table and your willingness to listen as long as the child is willing to talk. Or set aside a Sunday afternoon for tea and conversation with one friend, maybe one who's been having some difficulties lately, or one you haven't seen in a while.

And every now and then, you may wish to treat yourself to a private tea. Nothing special—just good tea well made, some toast maybe (take off the crust if you feel like it), and orange marmalade. Use company dishes and a pretty napkin. I find this an ever reliable antidote to writer's block, self-doubt, and rainy Saturdays.

## The Comfort of Safety

Probably the best feeling a home can have is one of safety, a sense that within its walls you're secure and protected. Of course the nature of life is risk, and perfect safety can never be guaranteed. Nevertheless, it is a great comfort to know that you and those you love are out of harm's way to the fullest extent possible.

In looking into safety at home, it's important to assess both how safe you *feel* and how safe you *are*. Since it's conceivable to feel safe in a place simply because it's familiar, critically assessing your home for its vulnerability to potential dangers such as fire and burglary is a valuable exercise. Many municipal fire and police departments will, at no charge, send an inspector to your home upon request to check for hazards and make recommendations. Departments lacking this service should be able to provide checklists for a do-it-yourself inspection.

A semiannual safety check—the same time you do your spring and fall simplification routines perhaps—is a good idea, too. Are your smoke detectors in working order? Are your fire extinguishers new enough and readily accessible? Is there an escape plan everyone in the family knows how to implement in case of fire? Are all your doors and windows still secure? Are your security lights operative? Have you reminded yourself lately to be alert when you go from your car to your house? Do you know your neighbors?

Neighbors who look out for one another or work together to form block patrols can greatly elevate the safety status of any area. Once my neighbors called to tell me that someone was taking pictures of my house—he turned out to be a real estate appraiser. Another time they left a message that a man had spent ten minutes outside my door. Even though the stranger was our piano tuner who had mistakenly come a day early, I was grateful that someone was paying attention.

In addition to vigilant neighbors, I have a security system, dead bolts, and a dog who is, to some degree, Doberman. My daughter and I have both taken Model Mugging, an intensive self-defense course. The result of all this is a feeling of safety, with solid backup behind the feeling. How safe do you feel where you live? What can you do to increase that feeling? Would you feel safer with window locks, an alarm system, a roommate, a different address? Which of these is feasible for you now and which can you work toward for the future? The privilege of feeling safe comes from facing the fear of danger and dealing with it head-on. Once done, feeling safe isn't a privilege anymore. You've earned it as a right.

## The Comfort of Correspondence

I met my friend Linda Adler as a pen pal when we were teenagers. She lived outside Washington, D.C., and later in New York. Linda's letters introduced me to new knowledge and fascinating people. She got me subscribing to *Women's Wear Daily* and *Dance* magazine and the *Village Voice*. She taught me about the stock market, which was her mother's business, and regaled me with stories of the celebrities she had an uncanny propensity for running into. We wrote for five years. Twenty years later she sent me a heavy package. In it were my letters, the history of my adolescence. At thirty-eight, I met the girl and young woman I had been—in my sealing wax stage, my small "i" phase, and my circular periods period.

Letter writing is less common now than when Linda and I were exchanging two or three substantial tomes each week. I've read that personal correspondence other than Christmas cards makes up only four percent of mail in America. We have many choices of ways to communicate besides writing letters, but letters, on stationery and in envelopes, offer a depth and dimension that a phone call or e-mail doesn't. For the writer, it's therapy, an opportunity to journal with a confidante. The heart and the hand have a truer connection than the heart and the mouth. That's why it's usually easier to write what we're feeling than to say it. That's why love letters are so special.

A letter is also intensely personal: It's addressed to you, sealed up, and anyone else's opening it is against the law. Letters are also personal in how they reflect the writer's choices in paper and stamps, typeface or handwriting. And letters last. They can be read over and over. If you become famous, your letters can make somebody rich. Even if you don't, they can make somebody smile. You can sign with "Love" even if you're too shy to say it, and you can call anyone on earth "Dear."

Receiving a letter is a genuine comfort, especially nowadays, when we're more likely to get a phone call. If there is a personal letter in my mail, I don't open it during the sober ordeal of sorting bills and discarding advertisements. I wait until I can be present with it, as I would want to be if the writer herself were sitting in a chair facing me.

Once read, I save personal letters in a basket devoted to that purpose. When I have time to write back, the letter is there to refer to. I don't feel obligated to answer most correspondence right away, though. There's enough to do that's time-sensitive. Letters are best answered when you feel moved to write. In that way, writing a letter can be as much of a comfort as reading one.

I keep my supplies for writing personal letters in a special box. My writing paper is here—banana fiber paper from Costa Rica, handmade rag paper from Nepal, tissue-thin airmail paper, and weighty traditional stationery. There are also cards and postal cards, and my letter-writing pen. It's not the same as those fast-moving pens I value for their efficiency in first drafts and note-taking. It's a fountain pen, reserved for personal letters. Having it in my hand puts me in the mood to write to a specific individual, to write something just for that person.

In those letters, I share what is going on in my life, what is going on in my head, how I'm thinking of the recipient, and what I wish for him. These letters aren't the novella-length ramblings I used to send to Linda, but they get their point across. Often I simply write a postcard. I had postcards printed with my name and address so I don't even have to write a return address in the corner. In the card's short space, and for reduced postage, I can let someone know she's on my mind and catch her up on my immediate goings-on. Although I get the most pleasure from writing letters at home with my fountain pen and my full attention, I also carry stamped postcards with me so I can do brief correspondence while I wait for appointments.

In addition to receiving and writing letters, there is comfort to be found in reading the letters of strangers with familiar names. There are collections of letters by Ernest Hemingway and James Joyce and Emily Dickinson. My favorite collection is Rainer Maria Rilke's *Letters to a Young Poet*. In one, he seeks to convey the concept of unconditional love, writing "Believe in a love that is being held for you like an inheritance and trust that in this love there is a strength and a blessing, out beyond which you do not have to step in order to go very far." If I thought I'd get to read something like that, I'd eavesdrop on other people's mail all the time.

## The Comfort of Getting Well

Although it was miserable to be sick, I remember the comfort of recovering from childhood maladies. Dede, the woman who lived with us as my caretaker, had remedies that would not be recommended for a sick child today: I got aspirin for nearly everything, butter and sugar for sore throats, and pot roast and potatoes as soon as I could eat. I was probably fourteen before I realized that pot roast wasn't standard fare for invalids.

Although I would change the particulars, I still long for that kind of attentive care when I'm under the weather. Some of it I get from other people; the rest I provide for myself. The rituals of healing *are* healing. In my childhood it was aspirin and pot roast; today it's ginger tea, spicy vegetable soup from my favorite Vietnamese restaurant, and a superb homeopathic flu remedy with the mouthful of a name, Oscillococcinum.

Have you ever stopped to think about your personal healing rituals? What medicine or herbs or vitamins do you swear by? What foods seem to give you strength when no others do, or do you feel best without solid food while you're recuperating? What do you read to feel better, and what do you think about?

One positive use for being sick is that it affords some time apart to rest the body and mind. We can palliate symptoms and keep going, but even one day at home, in bed, can be such a gift. It's like a short retreat when obligations must simply be put on hold. Besides, small illnesses attended to can forestall serious ones later, and the body has a miraculous ability to heal itself when it's allowed to rest.

The other side of the comfort of getting well is learning to provide that comfort for others. Some people seem to know this intuitively. I'm not one of them: I don't like feeling helpless and unable to make everything okay. It used to be terribly disconcerting to me when my daughter was sick and I could only give her medicine, make her juice, and replace empty tissue boxes. Then I thought of my own childhood and how the caring was more memorable than the cure. This helped me realize that I am neither a physician nor a shaman; my job is not to treat disease but to comfort someone I love. For my child, or anyone else, I can bring blankets, stories, food, and attention. It's not easy, because I have other commitments. I just don't have any others that are this important.

## Cultivating Comfort

When I'm feeling puny, I like to watch old films on video—like *Auntie Mame* and another that enchanted me as a little girl, *Bell, Book and Candle*. In it, Kim Novak played a contemporary witch who fell in love with a mortal and as a result began to take on the traits of ordinary humans. At one point, she gave her Aunt Queenie, who was also a witch, a scarf. Expecting some magical use for it, her aunt asked what the scarf *did*. Kim Novak replied, "Makes you look ravishing." Aunt Queenie was not impressed.

I used to be like that. I allowed myself a certain allotment of comforts as long as I could convince myself that they did something, that they had some purpose beyond making me happy. Now I am satisfied that making me happy is purpose enough. Happy people do most of the good on this planet. And even if they didn't, pure joy is respectable in its own right. It is the aim of spiritual practice and it is the reason, beyond such pragmatics as keeping warm and dry, for establishing a home.

Home *work* is serious stuff. This is where we confront our shadow side, our loneliness, and the people who can see through us when we least want to be transparent. This is where our words and actions are truly consequential. Regardless of how incidental we may be to several billion other people, to those in our household, we mean the world. This is a major responsibility. You *deserve* to read the comics or plant a rosebush, just for you.

Psychologist Abraham Maslow spoke of self-actualizing human beings as going from one peak experience to another. Tiny enjoyments are peak experiences of their own. We don't register

happiness based on how majestic something looks from the outside or how much it costs, but on how it touches us inside. That's
why it's unwise to compare where we live or how we live to someone else's situation. We see our lives from the inside out and theirs
from the outside in. The view is drastically different.

Maintaining a shelter for the spirit requires us to see our
homes and ourselves as clearly and directly as possible. So much
of modern reality isn't reality, it's retelling. We're assured that our
team scored the point when it comes back to us on the instant
replay. The words of the weather forecaster convince us that it's
cold outside with more validity than the frost on the windowpane.
The comforts of home, however, being largely interior and intimate, don't retell well. We have to experience them when they're
happening. If these comforts don't touch our hearts in the moment,
they never will in the recollection. That's because home comforts,
soul comforts, are not lifelike. They are life.

We savor life by expecting nothing and experiencing everything. When we go at high speed, we miss it. Some months ago I
remarked to my daughter how fast she's growing up. "Not really,"
she replied. "Thirteen years are a long time if you live them
slowly." Likewise, an evening or a Saturday or a three-day weekend is, when lived slowly, a luxuriously long time. Slow living
means paying attention. To pay attention to the comforts of home,
you first have to be there. Home provides basic comfort just
because it's home. For more than that, comforts need to be culti-
vated. This takes time. It takes being home enough for the beams
and rafters to know you live there. The world calls us away a lot
and there's good reason to go, but sometimes it is appropriate to
say, "Not this time. Tonight I'm staying home."

And when you do, invent some delight for yourself or for someone you love—even if the dishes are still in the sink and the bills are still in the mailbox. Bills and dishes are about the state of your house, a state that changes from day to day and moment to moment. You'll take care of them. But for now, take care of yourself, or of someone whose being is as valuable in your life as water and sunlight.

Giving some comfort to other people is an acknowledgment of their value. Giving a comfort to yourself is a nod to your soul that you know it's there and that you treasure it. Combining those you give to others and the ones you keep for yourself is like mixing flour and water for paste, or oil and vinegar for dressing: The combination becomes something new and useful. It creates from an apartment or from a house something far stronger and more meaningful than a physical structure. It creates a place of refuge, a place of contentment, the spiritual entity that sustains its residents today and years from now. It creates a home. There is no greater comfort.

# Afterword

In the year that passed between writing *Shelter for the Spirit* and seeing it in print, I retraced my steps to ensure that I was living everything I'd written—most of the time anyway. This was my preparation period before going out into the world—well, twenty-seven cities of it initially—to talk to actual people about what I'd put on paper.

My primary concern was how I felt about my own house. I'd come a long way toward loving and accepting it, but I wasn't certain I'd come far enough to stand in front of hundreds of people and say, "Do what I did." I was at a watershed. I meditated, made my lists, chronicled my soul needs, cooked in my tiny kitchen, and hosted lovely little celebrations at home at the slightest provocation. Finally, on a sunny September morning some seven months after I'd turned in the manuscript, I was sitting in my breakfast room when I realized that I was genuinely satisfied. My life was my art, my work was fulfilling, my daughter was thriving, and my home was the ideal backdrop for it all. My world could have been freeze-framed at that moment. I was blissfully content.

Do you know what happens when somebody is that content? An alarm sounds in the heavens and the angels get together and say, "Look! Over there—it's a content one. Do something, for goodness sake!" And they did. The following afternoon in a bagel shop I met William, the man I would marry thirteen months later.

Once we were engaged and discussing living space, it was apparent that neither my three-bedroom house nor his two-bedroom condo would accommodate this new family of two adults, four children, animals, and my office. It would take a remarkable house—something spacious but affordable. Where could we find a place like that? At the beginning of Chapter 6. The house I described with the ballroom on the top floor wasn't on the market, but I'd heard it was about to be. We bought it directly from the former owner.

My house also sold without advertising, to a neighbor's friend who had been "kicking herself for three years" that she hadn't bought the house before I did. It was no wonder that house never felt completely mine; in a way, it had been hers all along.

The wedding took place in our new home—not in the ballroom (that's my teenage daughter's teenage digs)—but before the living room fireplace. The house was decked with flowers, friends, and family. Since my husband and I have both lived in England and feel strong ties there, our reception was a British-style tea. His wedding gift to me was a watercolor of our new house with the inscription, "A Shelter for Our Spirit."

Now, I'm not implying that by simply accepting the place where you live and your life as it is you are guaranteed to find your true love and then move into a bona fide dream house. I am convinced, however, that accepting present circumstances as they are, yet persistently taking small steps to make them better, is indispensable to attracting more of the life you want.

That enhanced life, like the one preceding it, will be filled with opportunities to learn, serve, and grow. I'm gobbling humble pie as I realize that even though I wrote a book about home, I've married a man with twice my aesthetic sense and design ability. And after eighteen years as an only child and fourteen years as the parent of one, I'm stretching to learn to live as a large family when William's children are with us. I'm also accepting that my daughter is growing up. This house and this life are my dream come true, but she has her own dream: a studio walk-up somewhere in Greenwich Village to share with another theater student. In a few years, she'll be off fulfilling that dream, while I nurture this one.

Even miracles can be bittersweet, but living without them is too dreary to contemplate. Common miracles are the end point of taking the steps, everyday, that turn wishes into reality; self-created miracles have a way of accumulating until you wake up one morning with a life so rich you think you're the luckiest person on earth. That will make two of us.

# Appendixes

The four sections that follow explore ways in which some men and women are making even more committed connections with home. These include the people who spend much of their productive time there, with a home business, homeschooling their children, or both; and those who wish to experience life's most profound passages, birth and death, in the home environment.

Arranging your life to accommodate any of these, much less all of them, is in no way necessary for making your home your spiritual center, but those who do so believe it can help. Orese Fahey, a home-working and homeschooling mother from New Mexico, writes: "Instead of separating everything out into work, school, religion, home, we are trying to weave all these elements into a whole cloth, so that our family can experience learning, work, and spirituality throughout the day and throughout life." Bringing home activities that are usually associated with a school, an office building, or a hospital isn't something that everyone can do or that everyone wants to do. That there is a trend toward this, however, reflects the fact that all of us are taking home more seriously. We show this in ways that make sense to us, in ways that work in our individual and family lives. I think of home birth, homeschooling, working at home, or supporting a loved one who is dying at home as the advanced classes.

# Appendix A

## Home Birth

Having a baby at home is like playing a championship game in your own park. It isn't easy, but it's familiar. When a woman gives birth at home, she knows where things are. She can eat or get a glass of water without asking permission. She can walk around and see her own space, her favorite colors, her special possessions. She can sit, stand, squat, get on her hands and knees, scream, shout, and not give a hoot for rules or decorum. She can tap unrestricted the deep reserves of power stored for this momentous occasion.

Birth is a miracle wherever it happens. When it happens at home, the miracle is just a bit more intimate, a little less diffused than an equal miracle taking place in a hospital or birth center.

Before 1900, ninety-eight percent of Americans were born at home. By 1940, half of us still got to our first address without a commute from the hospital. By 1990, this figure had dropped to between two and three percent of births, but home birth is now on the upsurge. Its advocates cite statistics from The Netherlands, where thirty-eight percent of births take place at home and midwife-attended home birth gets the highest marks for safety. Moreover, medical and statistical studies from throughout the world show that for selected, healthy mothers, home birth results in lower cesarian rates, less fetal distress, fewer birth injuries, lower incidence of post-partum hemorrhage, and optimal family-infant bonding.

The parents who have brought childbirth home share the desire to be assured of a birth with the least intervention possible. For some, it is important to retain the option of having other family members and friends present at the birth, to allow the husband to "catch" the baby, or to avoid leaving a toddler to go off to the hospital and bring back an infant. Others simply want to take charge at this pivotal time.

"When I was pregnant with my first child, I heard about home birth and liked the idea," one woman told me, "but I was young and didn't even know anybody who breast-fed. When I was pregnant again at twenty-six, I knew I would do what I wanted. I planned every detail: finding a midwife, meeting her backup physician, getting all the supplies, enlisting friends to help. Actually, my labor went so fast I only called one friend, and the midwife got there five minutes after the birth. I never had any fear. I was empowered."

The aesthetic appeal of home comes into the decision for some couples as well. Birth centers and hospital birthing rooms are popular because they're homey, but they're not home. According to a mother whose two home births followed one in the hospital, "If you like where you live and you've made it comfortable, it's where you want the first feelings to happen. Even six hours later just isn't the same."

Home birth advocates also strongly contend that birth is not an illness to be treated but a process to be honored. This does not negate the physical and emotional criteria which need to be met for a low-risk home birth. The following questions provide a sample home birth screening:

Are you a nonsmoker in sound general health?

Have you been cleared by a physician as a good candidate for home birth?

Have you had quality, consistent prenatal care?

Have you eaten a healthy diet, taken the recommended prenatal vitamin/mineral supplements, avoided alcohol, and balanced regular exercise with plenty of rest throughout your pregnancy?

Have you read extensively and become educated about birth in general and home birth in particular?

Have you and your partner taken childbirth education classes (Lamaze, Bradley, etc.) and mastered the techniques taught there?

Do you have a qualified, experienced, dependable birth attendant (lay midwife, Certified Nurse-Midwife, or physician) to attend the birth? Are you clear on the financial costs involved? (A home birth is substantially less expensive than a hospital birth, but insurance copayment is sometimes difficult to get.)

Does your midwife have physician backup?

Does your birth attendant have hospital backup, preferably within twenty minutes of your house? Have you visited the hospital's facilities and found them acceptable? (Ideally, your backup hospital should be the one you would have chosen had you intentionally sought a hospital birth.)

Will your partner and/or a trained birth assistant be on hand to assist you through the stages of labor?

Is someone available to act as a *doula* (one who "mothers the mother") for the first two to four weeks following the birth? (Having someone at home to deal with cooking and household chores is equally important for a new mother who has had a hospital birth.)

Do you and your spouse agree on home birth?

Do you understand your state's laws regarding home birth? (Although many states allow home birth and its attendance by a physician, nurse-midwife, or lay midwife, others have archaic laws making attendance of a home birth by any of these professionals a criminal offense.)

Do you believe that having a healthy baby is always a "good birth," regardless of its circumstances?

If these questions can be answered affirmatively, a successful—indeed a *wonderful*—home birth is a most likely outcome.

For some couples, birth is a private affair, with only the birth attendant(s) invited. For others, relatives and friends gather to offer support during labor and share in the welcoming celebration for the baby. In either scenario, the heart of home birth is welcoming a new person into a home and into a family, with immediate bonding and no separation. The story of the birth itself becomes a part of family history, and its memory becomes a part of the character of a home. "The only negative thing I can say about my home births," said a mother of three, "is that you get so sentimental about the place where your children were born, it sure makes it hard when you want to sell your house."

# Helpful Books

Dancy, Rahima Baldwin. *Special Delivery: The Choices Are Yours.* Berkeley, Calif.: Celestial Arts, 1986.

Gilgoff, Alice. *Home Birth: An Invitation and a Guide.* Granby, Mass.: Bergin & Garvey Publishers, 1988.

Harper, Barbara, R.N. *Gentle Birth Choices: A Guide to Making Informed Decisions About Birthing Centers, Birth Attendants, Water Birth, Home Birth, Hospital Birth.* Rochester, Vt.: Healing Arts Press, 1994.

Jones, Carl. *Childbirth Choices Today: Everything You Need to Know to Plan a Safe and Rewarding Birth.* New York: Citadel Press, 1995.

Kitzinger, Sheila. *Homebirth: The Essential Guide to Giving Birth Outside of the Hospital.* New York: Dorling Kindersley, Inc., 1991.

Sears, William, M.D., and Martha Sears, R.N. *The Birth Book: Everything You Need to Know to Have a Safe & Satisfying Birth.* Boston: Little, Brown, 1994.

# Other Resources

Association for Childbirth at Home International, P.O. Box 430, Glendale, CA 91209. Trains and certifies childbirth educators, trains professional midwives, and offers seminars and advanced training for medical professionals. Also does research on statistical outcomes of home birth all over the world and has a speakers' bureau. Publications Department will provide free catalog of items offered for sale, including research papers, articles, printouts, and the workbook *Giving Birth at Home.*

*Mothering*, P.O. Box 1690, Santa Fe, NM 87504. Superb quarterly magazine for every stage of parenting and for parents-to-be. Contains regular section, "Pregnancy, Birth & Midwifery," which often addresses home birth. From its statement of purpose: "*Mothering* is both a fierce advocate of the needs and rights of the child and gentle supporter of the parents . . . recognizing that raising the heirs of our civilization well is the prerequisite for healing it."

La Leche League International, 1400 N. Meacham Rd., P.O. Box 4079, Schaumburg, IL 60168–4079. Mother-to-mother organization giving encouragement, information, and support to women who want to breast-feed. Meetings are held in homes throughout America and the world. A catalog of books including *The Womanly Art of Breastfeeding* and other publications on nursing, childbirth, and parenting is free upon request. LLL also publishes *New Beginnings*, a bimonthly journal for breast-feeding women, and holds a biennial international conference. Although La Leche League takes no stand on place of birth, my observation has been that a substantially higher percentage of home birth parents may be found among its members than in the general population.

NAPSAC (InterNational Organization of Parents and Professionals for Safe Alternatives in Childbirth), Rt. 1, Box 646, Marble Hill, MO 63764. Promotes education about natural childbirth; facilitates communication and cooperation among parents, health care professionals, and childbirth educators; encourages family-centered maternity care in hospitals; assists in establishment of maternity and childbearing centers; and helps establish safe home birth programs. Provides a free catalog of Mail Order Bookstore offerings, publishes quarterly *NAPSAC News* for members, and sponsors international conferences and local groups.

# Appendix B

## Homeschooling

Homeschooling is a growing phenomenon with a substantial history. Until the mid-1800s, learning at home was the norm and going to school full-time was "alternative." Now it's simply turned around. There are 15 million students in public and private schools in the United States, and an estimated 600,000 children who are homeschooled. Although based at home, these young people can cover a lot of territory. I know of some whose education includes exploring the country and sailing around the world. My own daughter, homeschooled since kindergarten, has done her fair share of traveling. When a dinner guest once said to her, "Well, Rachael, I guess you don't get report cards," another responded with, "No, she gets boarding passes."

When they're not seeing the world, homeschooled children and young people might be reading, composing music, programming computers, writing stories, walking in the woods, starting businesses, or playing, uninterrupted, for hours on end. You can get a taste of how homeschooling works by glancing at the classifieds in *Growing Without Schooling*, a popular publication for homeschoolers: "Free science magazine loaded with experiments," "Published poet offers mentoring (free) to teen homeschoolers via letters," "Travel to Jamaica ... Stay at our guesthouse with eleven-year-old boy and family."

Homeschooling families vary as much from one another as from their more conventionally educated peers. Typically, a homeschooling family is traditional: One parent, usually the father, works outside the home; the other parent is primarily in charge of educational activities. In some cases, two working parents arrange their hours to accommodate homeschooling, and single parents manage it by working at home or otherwise finding the resources that enable them to earn a living and teach their children.

A high percentage—probably half of homeschooling families—make the choice for religious reasons. These parents, usually conservative Christians, believe that teaching their own children is a right and obligation given them by God. They want their children to receive a Bible-based education without the humanism and liberality they see in public and secular schools.

Other homeschooling parents—some decidedly humanistic and liberal—take this route because they want their children to grow up free to follow their individual leanings and respect their innate learning styles. These parents in particular tend to favor experiential learning, the arts, and real-world experiences such as apprenticeships and mentoring situations. As one mother explained to me: "People who homeschool for religious reasons often want to protect their children from the world. People like me want to expose their children to more of the world than they'd get in school."

Today's homeschooling population is also burgeoning with children of all ages and parents of all persuasions who have been dissatisfied with other educational offerings and believe that, for all their children or one of their children, they can do better. When they start homeschooling, they discover a variety of ways to proceed. Some homeschoolers join with others for cooperative learning situations. Most are involved in some way with a local homeschooling organization that designs field trips and group classes.

In some families, school is re-created at home with desks and a blackboard and the Pledge of Allegiance, and school hours Monday through Friday from September to June. For others, much of the learning is integrated into life: There is math in measuring ingredients for a cake and playing a song on the piano. There is history at the art museum, on roadside markers, and in the tales of elders.

Packaged curricula, correspondence programs (traditional and computerized), secular and religious textbooks for homeschoolers, and classroom programs on video are available. However, many families employ these sparingly, preferring to take the world as their classroom. They like the term "unschooler," coined by the late educator and author John Holt. More recently, former teacher Grace Llewellyn, author of *The Teenage Liberation Handbook*, has defined "unschooler" as "one who learns from life and love and great books and late-morning conversations and big projects and eccentric uncles and mountains and mistakes and volunteering and starry nights—not from dull textbooks and sedative lectures and interfering homework."

When I heard that description, I wanted to shout "Bravo!" as if it had just been sung by Pavarotti. It called up memories from my own childhood. Although I liked school, I remember finding life before school far more interesting. That's when my grandmother told me stories and took me to the theater and taught me to read because I wouldn't leave her alone until she did. In life before school, I got to listen to grown-ups talk about religion and politics and say that the two things you should never talk about are religion and politics. I got to travel no matter what time of year it was. And I had all the time I needed to think and wonder and imagine. For me, that was early childhood. For homeschoolers, this is life.

The *amount* of life in homeschooling households is enormous.

Activities and projects are part and parcel of homes with children, but in those with homeschoolers, the energy is almost palpable. Something is always being discovered, created, discussed, figured out, planned, played, or explored. Nevertheless, homeschooling is still an uncommon choice. Those who hear of it for the first time have a litany of questions and concerns about the scholastic, psychological, and social ramifications of this rediscovered mode of learning. Among the most common are:

### *Is it legal?*

Yes. Some form of homeschooling is legal in every U.S. state and Canadian province, in Japan, Australia, New Zealand, Great Britain, and every other European country—with the exception of Germany. The laws vary from place to place, and simply crossing a state line can make a tremendous difference. In some states, parents are required to have a college degree in order to homeschool, or children may need to take periodic standardized tests or register with the local school district.

The best way to find out what the current legal requirements are where you live is to contact people who are already homeschooling. Any major homeschooling association or publication (see "Other Resources" at the end of this section) will put you in touch with groups or individuals in your area.

### *What about socialization?*

Homeschooling children are usually extremely well socialized because they associate with people of a variety of ages and interests. Without a classroom, the line between a fourth grader and a fifth grader blurs and children can simply be friends. Homeschoolers also spend more time with grown-ups and tend to see adults as real people. With their agemates, they form lasting friendships without the pressure to form cliques. And because these children have more time to spend with one another, they can become absorbed in creative play. If they're building a tree house or forming an ecology club or putting together a talent show, they can work on their project until it's finished.

Generally speaking, homeschooled children have about the same number of good friends as schooled children do; they just have fewer acquaintances. When kids don't go to school, they make friends through homeschooling groups, the neighborhood, classes they take (drama, art, dance, and the like), community and church activities, and pen pals. Homeschooled siblings tend to regard one another as friends as well.

In addition to spending time with others, children who learn at home generally have more time to themselves than other children do. This solitude is useful in defining one's life and discovering one's place in the world. Overscheduling is a modern peril for people of all ages, and its avoidance is especially important during childhood, when people are getting acquainted with themselves and their world. Because covering the academic bases does not take thirty hours a week in a one-on-one learning situation, there is extra time available for both being alone and being with others.

### *What qualifications do you need to be able to homeschool?*

In addition to meeting the legal requirements of your locality, you need to be able to provide an environment that stimulates learning. This may mean owning lots of books, games, and computer software, or simply having a well-used library card. You need to be comfortable in allowing art projects, science experiments, and theatrical productions to take place under your roof and, consequently, on your just mopped floors. You need to understand that learning is an innate propensity of the young, and trust that beyond what you specifically "teach," your children are learning a great deal by pursuing their own interests. Most of all, you need to be able to take children seriously and regard their work and play as important business.

### *How can homeschooled kids learn things their parents can't teach them?*

A basic premise among homeschoolers is that learning takes place all the time, throughout life, and in unexpected ways. When you're open to the myriad pathways by which learning can come into a life, you realize how many such pathways there are. Not everything must be formally taught and not every subject requires a teacher. Even young children can be autodidacts, or self-educators, on topics that interest them.

In addition, there are resources available for learning virtually anything. Among them are friends, mentors, tutors, other homeschooling parents, continuing education classes, camps, books, audiotapes, videotapes, computer software, educational TV, work-study programs, and college and junior college classes. An experience of this in my own family was finding a way to give my daughter the Chinese lessons she requested for her ninth birthday. First, we found a tutor through a private language institute. Two years later, she took a Chinese class at a local university. This was an actual college credit class that she was allowed to take as a noncredit student; this kept the cost low and her age was no barrier to being admitted.

### *What do homeschooled kids do about physical education?*

They tend to play for the joy of it and learn fitness activities that can continue into adulthood: hiking, biking, swimming, tennis, dancing, gymnastics, etc. Those who want to pursue team sports can do so through homeschool leagues and classes, community offerings, and in some cases their local schools. Because homeschooling parents pay school-supporting taxes, some have been allowed access to school athletic activities for their children.

### *How long will you homeschool?*

"As long as it works" is the answer you'll hear most often. Some parents homeschool young children and enroll them in school at age eight or nine when they feel their sons and daughters have the emotional maturity to successfully take this step. Others send their children to elementary school and homeschool from middle school on to lessen the peer pressure of the teen years. But homeschooling can start at any time and end whenever parents and children believe that going to school, or going back to school, would be advantageous.

Homeschooling is not necessarily an either/or proposition. Many highly respected figures throughout history were predominantly homeschooled but received some formal education. Writer Agatha Christie, for instance, had two years of high school; Benjamin Franklin had six months of formal schooling at age eight; Thomas Edison was in school for three months; Florence Nightingale was taught at home by her father until entering nurse's training as a young adult; Pulitzer Prize–winning author Pearl Buck was taught by her mother until age seventeen; composer Irving Berlin spent two years in school, but violinist Yehudi Menuhin only one day.

### *What about graduation and college?*

Most homeschoolers take the GED test for high school graduation. Some enroll in off-site or correspondence programs so that their diploma comes from the school with which they are affiliated, although they earn their credits at home. Local homeschooling groups offer commencement exercises and oftentimes a prom as well.

Homeschoolers do go to college, although many work, travel, or pursue some educational alternative first. (There is time for this since so many complete high school graduation requirements well before age eighteen.) They take standard college entrance exams. A rural California family, the Colfaxes, made news when they sent three homeschooled sons to Ivy League universities (see "Helpful Books," page 195), but homeschoolers are represented in a variety of colleges and universities. Some institutions actively seek them out, as they find homeschoolers to be mature, inventive, and a positive influence on campus.

### *What are the drawbacks of homeschooling?*

It's certainly not without its challenges. It takes serious parental commitment, but so does helping children through a more conventional education. To homeschool successfully, you have to enjoy the company of your children and be willing to both give them your time and allow them time on their own.

There is apt to be some financial sacrifice, since time spent helping children learn is time not spent in paid employment. Homeschooling itself has costs involved—field trips, music lessons, books, supplies, and assorted accoutrements, from educational games and math manipulatives to a microscope and a PC. (Homeschooling organizations help with curriculum fairs, sales of used books and equipment, and cooperative lending and research centers.)

Some homeschooling parents must contend with criticism from extended family. A father and mother may disagree on the choice, and homeschooling has been an issue in custody proceedings.

Homeschooled children can also be subject to the scrutiny of strangers ("Why aren't you in school?" "What's the capital of South Dakota?") and of other kids ("Do you have any friends?" "What do you do all day?"). Nevertheless, most homeschooled kids take the querying in stride. They seem to know that they are engaged in a wondrous process, one that has home as its center and no boundaries at all.

## Helpful Books

Colfax, David, and Micki Colfax. *Homeschooling for Excellence*. New York: Warner Books, 1988.

Guterson, David. *Family Matters: Why Homeschooling Makes Sense*. New York: Harcourt, Brace, Jovanovich, 1992.

Hegener, Mark, and Helen Hegener, eds. *The Homeschool Reader: Collected Articles from Home Education Magazine*. Tonasket, Wash.: Home Education Press, 1995.

Holt, John. *How Children Learn*. New York: Addison-Wesley, rev. ed., 1995.

————. *Learning All the Time*. New York: Addison-Wesley, 1989.

————. *Teach Your Own: A Hopeful Path for Education*. New York: Delacorte Press, 1981. (Note: This book is currently out of print but well worth a trip to the library.)

Llewellyn, Grace. *The Teenage Liberation Handbook: How to Quit School and Get a Real Life and Education*. Eugene, Ore.: Lowry House, 1991.

————, ed. *Real Lives: Eleven Teenagers Who Don't Go to School.* Eugene, Ore.: Lowry House, 1993.

Moore, Raymond, Ed.D., and Dorothy N. Moore. *The Successful Homeschool Family Handbook.* Nashville: Thomas Nelson Publishers, 1994.

Pride, Mary. *The Big Book of Home Learning*, vols. 1–4. Wheaton, Ill.: Crossway Books, Div., Good News Publishing, 1990.

## Other Resources

American Homeschool Association, P.O. Box 1125, Republic, WA 99166. Trade organization for homeschoolers and homeschool businesses; provides resources and directory services for homeschooling families; and works to provide information on this educational choice to those interested in homeschooling and to the general public.

*F.U.N. News*, 1608 Bellhaven Woods Court, Pasadena, MD 21122. Quarterly newsletter of the Family Unschoolers Network featuring articles by and for both parents and children. Free copy of newsletter and extensive "F.U.N. Books" catalog on request by mail or e-mail (210-8942@MCImail.com); web site provides sample newsletter and information (http.//members.aol.com/FUNNews).

"Genius Tribe: Tools for Unschoolers & Other Free People," P.O. Box 1014, Eugene, OR 97440. Catalog of resources for independent learners of all ages, especially older children, teenagers, and college-age people, from Grace Llewellyn, author of *The Teenage Liberation Handbook.*

*Growing Without Schooling,* Holt Associates, 2269 Mass. Ave., Cambridge, MA 02140. Bimonthly journal founded by the late John Holt; includes extensive input from homeschooling parents and children, directory of homeschooling families worldwide, and children's pen pal referral. "John Holt's Bookstore" catalog, providing resources for homeschoolers, is free upon request.

*Home Education Magazine*, P.O. Box 1083, Tonasket, WA 98855. Six issues per year containing articles, news, reader letters, resources, and reviews; will also send free catalog of magazine back issues and books published by Home Education Press.

The Moore Foundation, P.O. Box 1, Camas, WA 98607. International, Christian, nonprofit organization dedicated both to helping homeschoolers of all persuasions be more successful at the task, and to encouraging legislation friendly to homeschooling. Publishes bimonthly journal, *The Moore Report International*, and free catalog of materials supporting "The Moore Formula," a balanced educational style developed by Raymond Moore, Ed.D., and Dorothy N. Moore, that combines work, service, and academics.

National Homeschool Association, P.O. Box 157290, Cincinnati, OH 45215. National, nonprofit organization to advocate individual choice in education and serve homeschooling families; publishes quarterly journal, *The NHA Forum*, hosts annual conference, and provides networking and referral services.

Unschoolers Network, 2 Smith St., Farmingdale, NJ 07727. Information service for homeschoolers and potential homeschoolers. Will send upon request free four-page booklet on what one needs to do in order to homeschool, as well as a catalog of materials. Publications include thrice-yearly newsletter, *Unschoolers Network*, and fascinating booklet, *Famous Home Schoolers*, by Malcolm and Nancy Plent, the source of my information on well-known persons who learned at home.

# Appendix C

## Home Business

Buddha taught that enlightenment is achieved by living in accord with the Noble Eightfold Path, which calls for such practices as right speech, right meditation, and *right livelihood*. Right livelihood means making a living in a manner that provides a service, improves the lot of others, and expresses one's talents. In right livelihood, one also remembers that work is to provide for life, not overwhelm it.

Surely right livelihood can be pursued in a variety of locations: offices, factories, stores, and restaurants just begin the list. An increasing number of us are also finding home its fitting host. In working where we live, the nurturing ambience of the home environment is always available. The split between the personal and the professional becomes less pronounced. There's a feeling of integration and wholeness.

This is not an entirely new phenomenon. As recently as the late 1800s, ninety percent of Americans worked for themselves, most of them in their homes or on their land. The Age of Industry took us away from home, but the Age of Information is bringing many of us back. Home workers are found in an assortment of fields, but we have one thing in common: We're crazy about where we work.

I used to dress up and go to an office Monday through Friday from 9 to 5. Now I work at home from 8 to noon and any other free hours I get. I'm often in jeans and have a cat on top of my computer monitor or in my lap. I usually get a home-cooked meal for lunch and can almost always plan my work day around my daughter's activities. Sometimes I feel like the luckiest person on earth, but there are market research organizations estimating that I may have as many as 40 million at-home coworkers.

More than half of them have their own business in the tradition of cottage industry. The roster of a home business networking group in my area turned up people offering secretarial, legal, and dental services, computer support and computer repair, tax preparation, public relations, catering, child care, and pet care (grooming, walking, sitting—even a "vet without walls" who treats his patients on a house call basis). I was particularly taken with "Paper Chase," an international mail-order business selling hand-crafted stationery fashioned from junk mail, as well as kits so customers can make their own stationery.

The newest contingent of those employed at home are the telecommuters. Via fax and modem, they work at home full- or part-time for an employer company. This has made working at home an option for those who don't want to forgo the steady paycheck and health insurance that go with working for an established firm. Telecommuting has also legitimized home business in the minds of the public. Its reputation for being only a sideline or pin money operation has all but disappeared—as well it should: Even the President of the United States works where he lives.

The vast majority of professional homebodies, whether entrepreneurs or telecommuters, worked "out in the world" first. They have skills and they know how to market them. Some who are in business for themselves deal with their former employer on a per-job basis. Many headed home because of travel time, on-the-job stress, an independent nature, or having been downsized out of a job. A sizable contingent have come home to spend more time with their families. Mothers—and increasingly fathers—don't want to miss seeing their children grow up. Juggling work and parenthood can be less demanding when the juggling takes place in the same location.

For some families, finances make a home business more feasible than working away, saving the costs of commuting, a business wardrobe, lunches out, and child care. "Day care was eating us up," said a woman I interviewed who runs a home-based insurance agency with her husband. "This way, we save eight thousand dollars a year in day care for our two preschoolers. Since both of us work in the business, one of us is always available to be with the children."

Most people work to support a home and family. Working *in* the home and *with* the family brings a welcome cohesiveness. Children of home-working parents learn about earning a living firsthand. They're less likely than their peers to assume that money is a gift from ATM machines and unrelated to professional endeavors. Many home businesses are family businesses with everyone involved, but even when children just *see* their parents at work, they learn business principles. In modeling what they observe, these kids often come up with their own productive—and at times surprisingly profitable—enterprises. These include baby-sitting cooperatives, car-wash and housecleaning businesses, children's newsletters—and at least one subscription service for regular delivery of freshly baked bread.

Working at home not only affords closeness to the family but to the immediate community. When you both live and work in a neighborhood, you become doubly invested in its safety, beauty, and vitality. I've often noticed how empty and lifeless many upscale residential areas are. The houses are gorgeous, but there's nobody in them. Home workers join with full-time homemakers to create localities where somebody is at home. This is good news for neighborhoods and unfortunate for burglars.

A survey done by *Home Office Computing* described the typical home business person as forty-three years of age; fifty-eight percent were male, forty-two percent female; seventy-eight percent were married. About half of the home workers I interviewed dress every morning as if they had a train to catch, while others keep it casual. Most keep regular office hours, although the freedom to work at any hour is one they cherish.

Anyone new to working at home finds that there are rules to set and a routine to get used to. Will you have the TV on or off while you're working? Will you take personal calls during work time? If not, how will you screen your calls? What will you do about distractions and interruptions? These are problematic in an office setting, but then they're usually somehow related to your work. Interruptions at home more often have to do with deliveries, repair people, or somebody at the door wanting you to change religions.

Experienced home workers offer the following suggestions to those who want to join their ranks:

*Train yourself to work every day and stop every night.* People who have never worked at home tend to comment, "I don't have that much discipline. I'd never get anything done." The lure of personal and household commitments does exist, but overworking, rather than not working, seems to be a more widespread problem. Workaholism isn't found only in office buildings. The self-employed are particularly at risk for it: The entrepreneurial spirit is characterized by great acceleration and lousy brakes.

Those who maintain balance are able to work, take time away from work, and get back to it with minimal upset. They set hours based on life at home rather than the other way around. A woman with a home word-processing business, for example, says that watching her children step onto the school bus in the morning and seeing them get off it in the afternoon defines the parameters of her workday as surely as if she were punching a clock.

*Enlist the support of your family.* Many of the most successful undertakings are family businesses with both spouses taking part and the kids pitching in as they're able. If this is a solo venture, the people you live with at least need to see the benefits of what you're doing for the household as a whole. Although working at home can be an excellent way to be more available to those closest to you, it can sometimes seem to be taking you away from them in a way that working elsewhere didn't. When you're half an hour away, you're out of sight and probably out of mind. When you're down the hall asking not to be bothered, it can seem to others that you're simply ignoring them. Patience and some trial and error generally work out the kinks.

One woman I talked with had sold custom cotton clothing to supplement the family income. When she sat down with the numbers at the end of her first year, she realized that the income generated was not worth the time the business took from her children. In her case, the extra money was nice but not necessary; being with her kids took precedence. She liquidated the business and returned to full-time homemaking. A year later, though, she and her husband started another venture together, this one in long-distance communications. He is more involved in it than she is, so her primary emphasis can still be on her children and home, but with energy from both partners in the business, it's doing extremely well.

*Have separate office space and treat it as such.* This is good for something besides a tax deduction: It's visual proof that you're in business. Shutting the office door symbolically shuts out nagging house and yard chores—for the time being anyhow. Earmarking a room or rooms for business is also essential when the building where you fill the orders, meet the deadlines, and keep the books is also the one you count on to shelter your spirit.

This doesn't mean you never take work outside the office or that family members never come into it. A home business is just that: a home and a business sharing space, and each enriching the other.

*Get peer support from a networking group.* Networking groups for home-based businesspeople offer help over the rough spots. One man calls the group meetings his "coffee pot," the antidote to isolation. People in divergent fields find that, simply by being home-based, they are colleagues. You can locate a group through the American Association of Home-Based Businesses (see "Other Resources," page 205) or through a local university extension service.

*Be passionate about your work.* This helps wherever you're employed, of course, but when you bring your work into the sacred space of home, it needs to be work that you believe in and, ideally, work that you love. Sometimes, just being at home is enough to inspire passionate enthusiasm.

I think of bringing work into a home the way I would think of taking on a housemate. You wouldn't want a person living in your house who had totally different values from yours, someone you found boring or difficult to be around, or someone who interfered with your relationship with your family. Work done at home needs to meet the same criteria.

Home businesses often add employees and outgrow the house, and both the self-employed and telecommuters can attract the attention of a large company wanting to bring them on-site. People who have grown accustomed to working with all the comforts of home, however, don't readily give them up.

Marli Murphy had been working at home as a writer, editor, and humor columnist for almost three years. She loved the life, but was tempted by a job offer that included the insurance and retirement benefits she wasn't getting as a freelancer. After carefully weighing her options, she decided that being home was in itself a benefit that outweighed the others. She declined the offer. The company called her back, saying she could work from home with benefits. She became her company's first full-time employee to telecommute.

As in Marli's case, when working at home succeeds, it succeeds beautifully. It's still work, of course, complete with the inevitable problems, challenges, and setbacks. Even so, every day can be casual Friday and it's easy to get along with your boss.

## Helpful Books

Attard, Janet. *The Home Office and Small Business Answer Book: Solutions to the Most Frequently Asked Questions About Starting and Running Home Offices and Small Businesses.* New York: Henry Holt, 1993.

Berner, Jeff. *The Joy of Working from Home: Making a Life While Making a Living*. San Francisco: Berrett-Koehler Publishers, Inc., 1994.

Edwards, Paul, and Sarah Edwards. *The Best Home Businesses for the 90s: The Inside Information You Need to Know to Select a Home-Based Business That's Right for You*. New York: G. P. Putnam's Sons, 1994.

Eyler, David R. *Home Business Bible: Everything You Need to Know to Start & Run Your Successful Home-Based Business*. New York: John Wiley and Sons, Inc., 1994.

Whitmyer, Claude, and Salli Rasberry. *Running a One-Person Business*. Berkeley, Calif.: Ten Speed Press, 1994.

## Other Resources

American Association of Home-Based Businesses, P.O. Box 10023, Rockville, MD 20849. National nonprofit association dedicated to the support and success of home-based businesses across the country. Publishes quarterly newsletter, *The Connector*; has more than 100 chapters nationwide; offers prepaid legal services, and long-distance and travel discounts.

Barbara Brabec Productions, P.O. Box 2137, Naperville, IL 60567-2137. Provides free brochure on books and reports of interest to home business beginners.

*Home Office Computing*, Scholastic, Inc., 411 Lafayette St., New York, NY 10003. Monthly magazine for "Building Better Business with Technology."

Mothers' Home Business Network, P.O. Box 423, East Meadow, NY 11554. Provides information and support for mothers who choose to work at home; members receive newsletters

*Homeworking Mothers* and *Kids & Career*, plus a booklet with work-at-home ideas and start-up information, and an annual resource guide; brochure sent for stamped, addressed envelope.

Telecommuting/Telework Special Interest Group, International Teleconferencing Association, 1650 Tysons Blvd., Suite 200, McLean, VA 22102. Offers monthly audio-conference meetings; educational seminars; publications; networking opportunities; and *ITCA Communicator*, monthly newsletter of the umbrella organization, a professional society for those involved in integrative communications technologies.

# Appendix D

## The Final Passage

When Jacqueline Kennedy Onassis was released from the hospital to spend at home what was to be her last full day on earth, media attention was drawn to an event that is happening with increasing frequency among the less newsworthy: The final passage is coming home.

The spiritual impact of death at home is pronounced both for the person dying and for family members and friends. There is a dignity to leaving life unencumbered by technological interventions once it is certain these would only prolong the inevitable. There is an inherent rightness in letting go of this world from the place in it that is genuinely one's own. For those saying good-bye, a home death has a placidity lacking in a hospital or nursing home setting, with their cast of employees and the life-and-death dramas of other patients taking place all around.

When death routinely happened at home—as it did prior to 1900 and, in rural areas, up until World War II—it was accepted more as the natural and universal experience that it is. Death itself is different now. It used to be spread fairly evenly throughout the population, and included a substantial amount of infant mortality, young women dying in childbirth, and infectious diseases claiming people of all ages. Now, in spite of AIDS and other exceptions, death occurs primarily among the elderly. This allows the rest of us to put off thinking about it and look to modern medicine to keep it reserved for some far-off, hazy future. And since the majority of deaths occur in hospitals or nursing homes, most people other than medical personnel and clergy have never been present at the death of another human being. We learn about death and dying from university courses on the subject, a notion our great-grand-parents would have found most peculiar.

Even our pets are usually "put to sleep" in a veterinarian's office. When our dear cat Benjamin began to fail rapidly from cancer at the age of seventeen, I found a compassionate veterinarian to come to our house for the euthanasia. Benjamin left this life in his favorite straw basket, covered with Rachael's most prized possession, a fringed white scarf blessed by the Dalai Lama.

Although my personal experience with home death has been only that of our cat, more and more men and women are making the choice to die at home. This is an outgrowth of several factors:

Medical self-care and self-help in general: As people take more responsibility for their bodies, they are taking more responsibility for how they will leave them.

An aging population: Older people tend to be realistic about death and have given up denying its inevitability.

The AIDS epidemic: AIDS has brought death to more young people than could have been envisioned a generation ago. These individuals and their supporters have been adamant about the right to live while dying, through maintaining maximum quality of life until its end.

The changing face of health care: Government and private insurance providers are aware of the cost-effectiveness of caring for the terminally ill outside a hospital setting.

The hospice movement: Many people think of a hospice as a place to die, but it is rather an attitude toward death, a commitment to preserving the individual's comfort, dignity, and identity as a social being. Although in-patient hospices do exist in Britain, where the movement originated, and there are a few of these in the United States, hospice services—support for the terminally ill and their families—are far more frequently provided when the dying person is in a nursing facility or his own home.

The fact that these services are available—and that insurance and Medicare help pay for them—makes dying at home more feasible than it has been in recent history. In 1984 there were 31 hospices in the United States; in 1995 there were 1,795 such agencies.

While the goal of a hospital is to keep patients alive—by extraordinary methods if necessary—hospice honors the natural process of dying. It seeks to keep the dying person comfortable and pain-free, helps her deal with death on the psychological and spiritual levels, provides practical and psychological assistance to the primary caregiver and other family members, and assists survivors through the grief process. It uses medical intervention for the alleviation of pain and other unpleasant symptoms, not for the prolongation of life. People dying at home with hospice care are much less likely to have an IV, feeding tube, or other intrusive equipment that creates boundaries and keeps others physically and psychologically distant.

A primary focus of hospice is keeping the home death within this family framework. Hospice workers and volunteers fill in for the extended family that was available in earlier times to bolster those closest to the dying person. The job of primary caregiver is a twenty-four-hours-a-day responsibility. This person needs to be exceptionally compassionate, empathetic, and patient, as well as aware of his or her own limits and willing to get respite before reaching them. This is not a job to take on without support. Helping a dying person experience a "good death" usually requires a network of family, friends, and caring professionals who understand the hospice philosophy.

For a terminally ill person to be able to end his life in his own home, having made a living will in advance is ideal. A properly constructed living will, stipulating that no heroic life-extension measures be taken should a person reach terminal status, is a legally binding document. It ensures the dying person that his wishes will be carried out and saves the next of kin from having to "play God" and make such decisions for the person should he not be able to himself.

In deciding to die at home with hospice care, a person has chosen to accept intensive, supportive care physically, emotionally, and spiritually—including food, drink, medication to relieve pain and symptoms, conversation, touch, laughter, and whatever other pleasures she is able to enjoy. A hospice participant does not give up her right to reenter the hospital for better pain management or to give the primary caregiver a few days' rest. An individual may also revoke a hospice program at will, should she wish to return to an aggressive program aimed at cure rather than an equally aggressive one for symptomatic relief.

At a time earmarked by vulnerability, having choices puts the dying individual and the family in a position of strength. Physical recovery, although glorious when it happens, is not the only kind of healing. There is also healing in leaving from a place well chosen a life that has been well lived.

## Helpful Books

Ahronheim, Judith, M.D., and Doron Weber. *Final Passages: Positive Choices for the Dying and Their Loved Ones.* New York: Simon & Schuster, 1992.

Boerstler, Richard W., and Hulen S. Kornfeld. *Life to Death: Harmonizing the Transition*. Rochester, Vt.: Healing Arts Press, 1995.

Munley, Anne, I.H.M. *The Hospice Alternative: A New Context for Death and Dying*. New York: Basic Books, 1983.

Nearing, Helen. *Loving and Leaving the Good Life*. Post Mills, Vt.: Chelsea Green Publications, 1992.

Sankar, Andrea. *Dying at Home: A Family Guide for Caregiving*. Baltimore: The Johns Hopkins University Press, 1991.

Taylor, Joan Leslie. *In the Light of Dying: The Journals of a Hospice Volunteer*. New York: Continuum, 1989.

## Other Resources

Choice in Dying, 200 Varick St., New York, NY 10014. Organization advocating an individual's right to control his/her health care at the end of life. Provides for nominal fee state-specific living wills and medical powers of attorney. Also offers counseling service for persons in the midst of medical crisis whose wishes are not being honored.

Hospice Link, tel. 800/331-1620. A toll-free referral line (weekdays, 9:00 A.M. to 4:00 P.M. EST) providing the name, address, and phone number of the hospice nearest one's area, as well as general hospice information.

Hospice Association of America, 228 7th Street SE, Washington, D.C. 20003. Provides information about hospices in enquirer's locale, also information about what hospice is and guidance in understanding the concept and philosophy of hospice.

# Bibliography

Aslett, Dan. *Clutter's Last Stand: It's Time to De-junk Your Life!* Cincinnati: Writer's Digest Books, 1985.

Ban Breathnach, Sarah. *Mrs. Sharp's Traditions: Nostalgic Suggestions for Re-creating the Family Celebrations and Seasonal Pastimes of the Victorian Home.* New York: Simon & Schuster, 1990.

————. *Simple Abundance: A Daybook of Comfort and Joy.* New York: Warner Books, 1995.

Banchek, Linda. *Cooking for Life: Ayurvedic Recipes for Good Food and Good Health.* New York: Harmony Books, 1989.

Bender, Sue. *Every Day Sacred: A Woman's Journey Home.* San Francisco: Harper San Francisco, 1995.

Bennett, Julienne, and Mimi Luebbermann, eds. *Where the Heart Is: A Celebration of Home.* Berkeley, Calif.: Wildcat Canyon Press, and San Rafael, Calif.: New World Library, 1995.

Berthold-Bond, Annie. *Clean & Green: The Complete Guide to Nontoxic and Environmentally Safe Housekeeping.* Woodstock, N.Y.: Ceres Press, 1990.

Brother Lawrence of the Resurrection. *The Practice of the Presence of God.* New York: Paulist Press, 1978.

Cahill, Mary Ann. *The Heart Has Its Own Reasons: An Inspirational Resource Guide for Mothers Who Choose to Stay Home with Their Young Children.* New York: New American Library, 1983.

Carlson, Richard, and Benjamin Shield, eds. *Handbook for the Heart.* Boston: Little, Brown, 1996.

————. *Handbook for the Soul*. Boston: Little, Brown, 1995.

Chopra, Deepak, M.D. *Journey Into Healing: Awakening the Wisdom Within You*. New York: Harmony Books, 1994.

————. *Perfect Health: The Complete Mind/Body Guide*. New York: Harmony Books, 1991.

Cunningham, Scott, and David Harrington. *The Magical Household: Empower Your Home with Love, Protection, Health and Happiness*. St. Paul, Minn.: Llewellyn Publications, 1993.

Dominguez, Joe, and Vicki Robin. *Your Money or Your Life: Transforming Your Relationship with Money and Achieving Financial Independence*. New York: Viking, 1992.

Ellsworth, Robert, and Janet Ellsworth. *Prayers That Work*. New York: Putnam Publishing Group, 1997.

Evans, Noella. *Meditations for the Passages and Celebrations of Life: A Book of Vigils*. New York: Bell Tower, 1994.

Goldbeck, David. *The Smart Kitchen: How to Design a Comfortable, Safe, Energy-Efficient, and Environmentally Friendly Workspace*. Woodstock, N.Y.: Ceres Press, 1989.

Heffern, Rich. *Adventures in Simple Living: A Creation-Centered Spirituality*. New York: The Crossroad Publishing Co., 1994.

Huxley, Aldous. *The Perennial Philosophy*. London: Chatto & Windus, 1969.

Jones, Susan Smith. *Choose to Live Each Day Fully: A 365-Day Guide to Transforming Your Life from Ordinary to Extraordinary*. Berkeley, Calif.: Celestial Arts, 1994.

Kimmel, Tim, and Darcy Kimmel. *Little House on the Freeway: 301 Ways to Bring Rest to Your Hurried Home*. Sisters, Ore.: Multnomah Books, 1994.

Lee, Harper. *To Kill a Mockingbird*, 35th Anniversary Edition. New York: HarperCollins Publishers, 1995.

Lingerman, Hal A. *The Healing Energies of Music*. Wheaton, Ill.: Quest Books, 1983.

Millman, Dan. *The Laws of Spirit: Simple, Powerful Truths for Making Life Work*. Tiburon, Calif.: H. J. Kramer, Inc., 1995.

Mitchell, Paulette. *The Fifteen-Minute Vegetarian Gourmet*. New York: Macmillan, 1987.

Moore, Thomas. *Care of the Soul: A Guide for Cultivating Depth and Sacredness in Everyday Life*. New York: HarperCollins, 1992.

————. *The Re-enchantment of Everyday Life*. New York: HarperCollins, 1996.

Mundis, Jerrold. *Earn What You Deserve: How to Stop Underearning and Start Thriving*. New York: Bantam Books, 1995.

————. *How to Get Out of Debt, Stay Out of Debt, and Live Prosperously*. New York: Bantam Books, 1988.

Nhat Hanh, Thich. *The Miracle of Mindfulness: A Manual on Meditation*. Boston: Beacon Press, 1992.

————. *Peace Is Every Step: The Path of Mindfulness in Everyday Life*. New York: Bantam Books, 1991.

Norris, Gunilla, with photographs by Greta D. Sibley. *Being Home: A Book of Meditations*. New York: Bell Tower, 1991.

Peace Pilgrim. *Peace Pilgrim: Her Life and Work in Her Own Words* ("compiled by some of her friends"). Santa Fe, N.Mex.: Ocean Tree, 1983.

Pipher, Mary, Ph.D. *The Shelter of Each Other: Rebuilding Our Families*. New York: Putnam Publishing Group, 1996.

Rasberry, Salli, and Padi Selwyn. *Living Your Life Out Loud: How to Unlock Your Creativity and Unleash Your Joy*. New York: Pocket Books, 1995.

Reynolds, Dana, and Karen Blessen. *Be an Angel: Heavenly Hints for Angelic Acts from Your Guardian Spirits*. New York: Simon & Schuster, 1994.

Robbins, John. *May All Be Fed: Diet for a New World*. New York: William Morrow & Co., Inc., 1992.

Rossbach, Sarah. *Interior Design with Feng Shui*. New York: Arkana, 1991.

Sanders, Darcie, and Martha M. Bullen. *Staying Home: From Full-Time Professional to Full-Time Parent*. Boston: Little, Brown, 1992.

Scott, Anne. *Serving Fire: Food for Thought, Body, and Soul*. Berkeley, Calif.: Celestial Arts, 1994.

Stoddard, Alexandra. *Creating a Beautiful Home*. New York: Avon Books, 1992.

Venolia, Carol. *Healing Environments: Your Guide to Indoor Well-Being*. Berkeley, Calif.: Celestial Arts, 1988.

Visser, Margaret. *Much Depends on Dinner: The Extraordinary History and Mythology, Allure and Obsessions, Perils and Taboos of an Ordinary Meal*. New York: Collier Books, 1986.

Williamson, Marianne. *Illuminata*. New York: Random House, 1994.

Yogananda, Paramahansa. *Metaphysical Meditations*. Dallas: Amrita Foundation, 1993.

Zukaw, Gary. *The Seat of the Soul*. New York: Fireside, 1989.

For information on the author's workshops and seminars in your area, please write to:

Victoria Moran
P.O. Box 3344
Kansas City, KS 66103

Kindly include a self-addressed, stamped envelope.